UNDERSTANDING ANDRE DUBUS

UNDERSTANDING CONTEMPORARY AMERICAN LITERATURE

Matthew J. Bruccoli, Founding Editor

Linda Wagner-Martin, Series Editor

UNDERSTANDING
ANDRE DUBUS

Olivia Carr Edenfield

The University of South Carolina Press

Published by the University of South Carolina Press
Columbia, South Carolina 29208

www.sc.edu/uscpress

Manufactured in the United States of America

26 25 24 23 22 21 20 19 18 17 10 9 8 7 6 5 4 3 2 1

Library of Congress Cataloging-in-Publication Data

Names: Edenfield, Olivia Carr, author.
Title: Understanding Andre Dubus / Olivia Carr Edenfield.
Description: Columbia : The University of South Carolina Press, 2017. | Series: Understanding contemporary American literature | Includes bibliographical references and index.
Identifiers: LCCN 2016054276 (print) | LCCN 2016054336 (ebook) | ISBN 9781611177404 (hardcover : alk. paper) | ISBN 9781611177411 (ebook)
Subjects: LCSH: Dubus, Andre, 1959– —Criticism and interpretation.
Classification: LCC PS3554.U2652 Z59 2017 (print) | LCC PS3554.U2652 (ebook) | DDC 813/.54 [B] —dc23
LC record available at https://lccn.loc.gov/2016054276

This book was printed on a recycled paper with 30 percent postconsumer waste content.

For my parents, Paul and Rose Watkins Carr, and my husband, Daniel Edenfield, with love

"I am fixed in transition, static, pulled one way by my youth, and the other way by what I have learned since then."

Andre Dubus, "Of Robin Hood and Womanhood," *Broken Vessels*

"Sacraments are myriad."

Andre Dubus, "Sacraments," *Meditations from a Moveable Chair*

CONTENTS

SERIES EDITOR'S PREFACE

The Understanding Contemporary American Literature series was founded by the estimable Matthew J. Bruccoli (1931–2008), who envisioned these volumes as guides or companions for students as well as good nonacademic readers, a legacy that will continue as new volumes are developed to fill in gaps among the nearly one hundred series volumes published to date and to embrace a host of new writers only now making their marks on our literature.

As Professor Bruccoli explained in his preface to the volumes he edited, because much influential contemporary literature makes special demands, "the word understanding in the titles was chosen deliberately. Many willing readers lack an adequate understanding of how contemporary literature works; that is, of what the author is attempting to express and the means by which it is conveyed." Aimed at fostering this understanding of good literature and good writers, the criticism and analysis in the series provide instruction in how to read certain contemporary writers—explicating their material, language, structures, themes, and perspectives—and facilitate a more profitable experience of the works under discussion.

In the twenty-first century Professor Bruccoli's prescience gives us an avenue to publish expert critiques of significant contemporary American writing. The series continues to map the literary landscape and to provide both instruction and enjoyment. Future volumes will seek to introduce new voices alongside canonized favorites, to chronicle the changing literature of our times, and to remain, as Professor Bruccoli conceived, contemporary in the best sense of the word.

Linda Wagner-Martin, Series Editor

ACKNOWLEDGMENTS

I read my first short story by Andre Dubus when I was a graduate student at the University of Iowa in the mid-1980s. I had heard about his fiction from my husband, Daniel, who was a member of the undergraduate Writer's Workshop, where Dubus is revered. When I finished "Leslie in California," I knew I had received a gift. I had no idea just how blessed I would become.

In 1992 I called Dubus's publishing house, David R. Godine, in Boston, seeking an interview with the writer, which he granted me in February of that year. When we met, "The Colonel's Wife" had just appeared in print, his first story written in full since his accident in 1986. Over the weekend, we talked through *Selected Stories,* and what I remember now more than what he said was the way he made me feel, that my time was important, my work of consequence, though I had little idea what I might do with our hours of conversation. I spent the summer transcribing the interview, then put it in a drawer.

A few years later, I began work on my Ph.D. at the University of Georgia, where I wrote my dissertation on Dubus's short fiction. James Nagel, my mentor to this day, directed my project, and I am grateful for his consistently sound guidance and friendship. I supplemented the reviews and scant criticism with my interview and conversations the writer had had with others, such as Thomas E. Kennedy, the first to write a book-length study of Dubus's fiction and the most prolific of the scholars devoted to his work. Kennedy's essays, along with those by Patrick Samway, S.J., remain the best of the criticism, and both critics continue to influence my reading. I am indebted to their keen insights.

In 2007 I put together a panel honoring Dubus's work for the American Literature Association's annual conference in Boston. Donald Anderson suggested that I contact Andre III—"the nicest man you will ever meet," he said. I am grateful to Donald for his recommendation; it changed my life. And he was right about Andre. He took time away from his very busy schedule to sit on that panel and then to serve as keynote speaker in the fall of 2008 for the American Literature Association Symposium on Fiction, which I directed in Savannah,

Georgia. At that symposium, my friends Kirk Curnutt and Alfred Bendixen encouraged me to ask Andre III about writing his father's biography. Andre III and his sister Suzanne Dubus share the responsibilities of their father's literary estate, and thankfully the two said yes to my request. That led to a book of interviews and now to this project, with the biography to follow.

I am grateful to the Dubus family, each one of them, for their patience and support and friendship. Andre III; his wife, Fontaine; Suzanne; and Jeb are tender mercies. Their generosity is unlimited; their willingness to bring me into their lives and trust me with their father's legacy is sometimes simply overwhelming. Each of Andre's six children was cut from the same cloth: they are artistic, spiritually and physically beautiful, generous, and pure of heart. Pat Dubus remains as lovely as she was the day Andre married her, with a soul open and responsive to the joys of life. She is as good a woman as I could ever hope to be, and I am grateful for her friendship and constant encouragement. Andre's third wife, Peggy Rambach, is equally kind, generous, and supportive, and we have spent many happy hours together discussing her years with Andre. I have had the blessing, too, of spending time with my dear friend Kathryn, Andre's oldest sister. I will cherish those October days we spent driving the roads of the Louisiana bayou as she talked about her life as a Dubus, her love for her brother, his art. The connections she made for me are priceless. I spent time in New York with Philip Spitzer and witnessed firsthand his love for Andre, his dear friend and "brother." David Godine, that wise man, met me in Boston to talk about his decision to publish Dubus's work, their respect for each other, and Andre's loyalty. People are known by the company they keep; having met Andre's company, I know that he was a blessed man. There are too many to name here, but no people could be finer than the family and friends of Andre Dubus.

I remain appreciative of Alfred Bendixen, executive director of the American Literature Association, for his friendship and his unwavering belief in my work. I thank my sisters, Elizabeth Carr Edwards and Paula Carr Cain, and my sister-in-law, Becki Edenfield, who have helped in countless ways. Richard and Dorothy Mugavero and Bob Peters watch over me like family when I am in Newburyport; their open hearts make me feel at home. I am grateful, too, for the support of Georgia Southern University and the Department of Literature and Philosophy for financial resources and the time to work on various projects related to Dubus. Thank you to Walter Biggins, formerly of the Conversations series at University Press of Mississippi, for allowing me the privilege of editing their collection of Andre's interviews. I am especially grateful to Linda Wagner-Martin, editor of this series, for her patience and guidance during this project. My mother passed away in 2014, and I will never forget Linda's kindness and support as I struggled with my grief to meet this deadline.

I am blessed to have had such supportive parents, Rose and Paul Carr, whose sensitive hearts were full and loving. I remain in all things most grateful to my dear family, my husband, Daniel, and our children, Cohen and Rose, who have patiently supported my every effort. Each day with them is precious, as Andre's work confirms. I trust I am better for his gifts.

CHRONOLOGY

1936 Born on August 11 to Andre Jules (November 16, 1904) and Katherine (Burke) Dubus, (January 2, 1903) in Lake Charles, Louisiana. Welcomed by two older sisters, Kathryn Claire (November 3, 1930) and Elizabeth Nell (October 26, 1933).

1944 Enters the Christian Brothers School, Lafayette, Louisiana.

1954 Graduates from the Christian Brothers High School.

1958 Earns B.A. in English and journalism from McNeese State College, Lake Charles, Louisiana. Marries Patricia Lowe, February 22. Commissioned as lieutenant in U.S. Marine Corps. Birth of daughter Suzanne Catherine Dubus, August 16.

1959 Birth of son Andre Jules Dubus III, September11.

1960 Birth of son John Ethan Burke Dubus (Jeb), November 29.

1963 Birth of daughter Nicole Mignon Dubus, February 3. Death of Andre Sr. Publishes "The Intruder" in *Sewanee Review.* Resigns commission from U.S. Marine Corps as captain.

1964 Enters M.F.A. program in fiction, University of Iowa, Iowa City, Iowa.

1966 Completes M.F.A., University of Iowa. Accepts teaching position with the English Department at Bradford College, Bradford, Massachusetts.

1967 Publishes *The Lieutenant* with Dial Press.

1970 Divorces Patricia Lowe Dubus. Publishes "If They Knew Yvonne," selected for *Best American Short Stories, 1970.*

1975 Publishes *Separate Flights.* Receives *Boston Globe* first annual Laurence L. Winship Award. Marries Tommie Gale Cotter in June.

1976 "Cadence" selected for *Best American Short Stories, 1976.* Receives a Guggenheim Fellowship.

1977 Publishes *Adultery and Other Choices.*

1978 Receives National Endowment for the Arts grant. Divorced from Tommie Gale Cotter in June. "The Fat Girl" selected for annual Pushcart anthology.

1979 "The Pitcher" selected for *Prize Stories: The O. Henry Awards.* Marries Peggy Rambach, December 16.

1980 Death of Catherine (Burke) Dubus Watkins, age seventy-eight. "The Winter Father" selected for *Best American Short Stories, 1981*. Publishes *Finding a Girl in America: A Novella and Seven Short Stories.*

1982 Birth of daughter Cadence Yvonne Rambach Dubus, June 11.

1983 Publishes *The Times Are Never So Bad: A Novella and Eight Short Stories.*

1984 Retires from Bradford College. Publishes *Voices from the Moon.* Publishes *We Don't Live Here Anymore: The Novellas of Andre Dubus.*

1985 Receives National Endowment for the Arts Literature Fellowship. Publishes limited edition of *Land Where My Fathers Died.*

1986 July 23, struck by car driven by Nancy Anthony of Woburn, Massachusetts, on Route 93 in Wilmington, Massachusetts, after stopping to assist an accident victim on his way home from Boston's Combat Zone, where he was conducting research for a story. Lost his left leg above the knee with extensive surgeries on the right leg to follow. Did not regain ability to walk. Reprints *The Lieutenant* as paperback with Green Street Press. Receives Guggenheim Fellowship. Publishes *The Last Worthless Evening: Four Novellas and Two Short Stories.*

1987 Birth of daughter Madeleine Elise Rambach Dubus, January 10. In October, his wife, Peggy Rambach, moves out of the couple's Haverhill home with daughters Cadence and Madeline. Publishes *Blessings.*

1988 Suffers a mild heart attack, October 30. Receives the Jean Stein Award from the American Academy and Institute of Arts and Letters and the MacArthur Foundation Fellowship. Publishes *Selected Stories.* Publishes an edited collection of stories, *Into the Silence.*

1991 Receives the PEN/Malamud Award for Excellence in Short Fiction. Publishes *Broken Vessels.*

1992 *Broken Vessels* finalist for Pulitzer Prize.

1996 Winner of the Rea Award for the Short Story. Publishes *Dancing After Hours* with Alfred A. Knopf.

1998 Publishes *Meditations from a Moveable Chair.*

1999 February 24, dies of heart failure at home in Haverhill. Buried April 13, 1999, Fenway Park's opening day. Sons Andre III and Jeb and their best friend, Bill Cantwell, dig the grave. The Red Sox beat the Chicago White Sox 6–0.

2001 Todd Field adapts "Killings" into the film *In the Bedroom,* nominated for five Academy Awards, including Best Picture. Posthumously publishes *In the Bedroom,* a selection of previously published stories, including "Killings." Loyola University Maryland hosts a conference focused on

Dubus's works. The revised proceedings are published in *Religion and the Arts.* Xavier Review Press publishes a collection of essays honoring Dubus and his work, *Andre Dubus: Tributes,* edited by Donald Anderson.

2003 Xavier Review Press publishes collection of interviews *Leap of the Heart: Andre Dubus Talking,* edited by Ross Gresham.

2004 Screenwriter Larry Gross adapts "We Don't Live Here Anymore" and "Adultery" into the film *We Don't Live Here Anymore,* directed by John Curran.

2009 *The Times Were Never So Bad: The Life of Andre Dubus,* a film directed by Edward J. Delaney, is released by Backspace Pictures.

2010 Saint Anselm College hosts a conference on the work of Andre Dubus and Andre Dubus III, April 8–10. *Xavier Review* publishes a special issue of the conference proceedings.

2013 University Press of Mississippi published a collection of interviews *Conversations with Andre Dubus,* edited by Olivia Carr Edenfield.

CHAPTER 1

Understanding Andre Dubus

Andre Jules Dubus Jr. was born in Lake Charles, Louisiana, on August 11, 1936, to Andre and Katherine Burke Dubus. His mother was a Catholic, and, over the years, her son developed a deep love for the faith. His Catholicism was a determining factor in his life, and along with his seven-year service to the Marine Corps and his three marriages, his religion had a profound effect on his fiction. The youngest of three children, Andre was adored by his two older sisters, and perhaps his close relationship to the women in his family, his mother included, provided the foundation for his profound ability to write empathetically from a female perspective. The family moved to Baton Rouge in 1939 and then to Lafayette in 1944, where they would remain until his father's job promotion sent the family back to Lake Charles when Andre was a senior in high school. Not wanting to leave his graduating class, Andre stayed behind in Lafayette, living with a good friend who was the leader of their group. The young Andre was never quite in sync with this fairly rough knot of boys from prominent families in what was then a small, segregated town of twenty-five hundred people. Atypical of most boys his age, he had a heightened sensitivity to the issues of class and racial disparity prominent in the Deep South of the 1940s. Wanting to fit in with his peers, uncertain and self-conscious, he kept his political opinions to himself until they found an outlet in his writing.

His boyhood days were influenced in part by his mother's love of the arts. He was an avid reader, and his small frame and distaste for violence put him on the periphery of his social circle. While his friends would gather on Saturday and box one another in a fairly elaborate system of weight class and betting, Andre hung back, watching, never a fighter himself, though violence would be prevalent in many of his works. In fact, sixteen of his fifty-eight stories, a full fourth of his canon, are crime narratives. Though he loved and wrote lovingly about baseball, he gravitated to his school newspaper at the Christian Brothers School rather than the team sports that occupied most of his friends' time. Andre was shy, a word he would use over and over to describe himself, even after he became a notable writer of short fiction. This reticence sprang in part from his lack of physical confidence and a fear that he never quite measured up to be the boy his father expected, a conflict that appears in many of his stories about boyhood in Louisiana.

When Andre graduated from high school, Andre Sr., came to collect him to take him back to Lake Charles, where he would spend the summer before enrolling in college. His advisor told the senior Dubus that his son had a talent for writing, and when Andre Jr. tried to play down the praise, he was surprised by his father's supportive reaction. As Dubus would share in a 1984 interview with Kay Bonetti, his father had asked his teachers at the Christian Brothers school what his son "was good for, and they said English and writing. Well in the fifties, we used to say 'Big deal. So what.' I said, 'Big deal.' He said, 'It's a good living.' And my heart leaped. And that's when I knew that I wanted to write, and I went home and started writing stories. Because I always wanted his approval" (Edenfield 56).

The quiet, respectful boy was an observer, and in small-town Louisiana there was much to observe. The Jim Crow laws that dominated the South and divided the town's black and white citizens had a profound effect on Andre's view of his birthplace. He was deeply ashamed of the prejudice he witnessed and made a name for himself on the McNeese State campus, where, majoring in English and journalism, he spoke out against social injustice in his weekly column, "The Way I Feel," written for the college newspaper. The sensitive, perceptive young man had found an outlet for the opinions that he had long kept to himself. In 1958 Dubus graduated after having married in February of that same year the beautiful, highly intelligent Patricia Lowe. Hoping at last to please him and to measure up to the man he believed his father wanted him to be, Andre Jr. joined the Marine Corps. The validation of his writing that he had once felt from his father had been short lived. Though he would never live in the South again except for two brief teaching appointments, he carried with him a devotion to his faith that influenced his life choices and his writing. The ritual of the Catholic Church provided a ballast during some of the more challenging events of his life while at the same time it contributed to his conflicted sense of self.

The young couple lived along the West Coast in military housing, where Pat gave birth to four children in six years. Dubus would eventually earn the rank of captain. His years as a marine influenced his short fiction and essays and served as the basis for his first novel, *The Lieutenant,* published by Dial Press in 1967. The main character, Dan Tierney, a thinly veiled Dubus, contests charges of indecency brought against four marines in his command. The novel was praised for its style and for its courage in confronting with honesty and empathy what was for the times a highly controversial subject.

In 1963 Dubus received the news that his father was gravely ill. He returned home to Louisiana and was with his family when his father passed away. He admitted to Bonetti that his reaction to his father's death was conflicted: "When he finally died of cancer at home, I said thank God. I thought it meant because finally the pain is over. It did. It also meant now I'm no longer the sissy he's ashamed of. I'm me, but I didn't digest all of this. I went back as a Marine, expecting to do twenty years, only to resign in two months" (Edenfield 57). Though he had joined the service to gain his father's respect, the senior Andre's death freed his son finally to become the fiction writer he was always meant to be. He had continued to write stories and, in fact, published his first, "The Intruder," in the *Sewanee Review* the same year his father died. The coincidence is profound.

On his wife's recommendation, he resigned the security of his commission and moved his family to Iowa City, Iowa, where he began his M.F.A. in creative writing at the University of Iowa as part of their prestigious Writers' Workshop. He was mentored by Richard Yates and was a Brown Street neighbor of Kurt Vonnegut. Though the couple was only in Iowa City for two and a half years, they were formidable times. Dubus was the first M.F.A. student to publish a novel while still in the program. A disciplined writer and teacher, he needed isolation and quiet to craft the short stories for which he is known, and his wife provided that for him. Though Pat was equally influenced by the progressive climate of university life, she had carryover ideas from the 1950s South about her responsibilities as a wife and mother, and on the surface the couple seemed very conventional. Financially hard as the times were, they were perhaps the happiest two years of the family's life together in spite of troubling martial conflicts, which would serve as entry points into his works of fiction that contend with families in crisis.

In 1966 Dubus began teaching literature and creative writing at Bradford College and remained on faculty, in spite of more lucrative offers from other universities, until mental and physical exhaustion forced him to seek early retirement in 1984. Dubus's divorce in 1970 from his first wife and his separation from his children have been made public by his award-winning novelist son, Andre III, in his 2011 memoir, *Townie.* Dubus would remain a distant but loving father, leaving his children and ex-wife to struggle along much on their own devices. According to Andre, their divorce was amicable. As he would tell

Bonetti, "I had a wonderful first wife. . . . Our marriage didn't make it because we were nineteen and twenty-one in the fifties. She was pregnant; we got married. You will notice if you look closely that the ex-wives in my stories are wonderful because they're all based on her because we had a splendid divorce" (Edenfield 57). In truth, however, Dubus's involvement was limited to scheduled visits that substituted for family life and which in no way contributed to his children's sense of discipline or security, though all of his and Pat's offspring, as well as Pat herself, would go on to be highly successful and respected professionals in their fields. The Allison/Linhart stories as well as his novel *Voices from the Moon* confront such issues of parental abandonment.

After a brief marriage in 1975 to his college sweetheart, Tommie Gale Cotter, the unhappy and badly matched couple divorced. By then, Dubus was already in love with his third wife, Peggy, whom he married less than two years after their meeting at Godine, the small, high-quality publishing house in Boston to which Dubus remained loyal for most of his publishing career.[1] Dubus was twice his young wife's age, and though the two were connected by their writing, the strain of their age and class differences led to constant fighting. Peggy was pregnant with their second daughter when tragedy struck the family in profoundly disturbing ways from which they would never fully recover.

Coming back from Boston, where he had been conducting research for a story he was writing, the ex-marine stopped along I-93 in Wilmington, Massachusetts, just after midnight on July 23, 1986, to aid Luz Santiago and her brother, Luis, who were stranded after running over an abandoned motorcycle. While assisting the two across the highway, Andre and Luis were struck by a car driven by a young woman who was confused by the taillights. The impact left Dubus on the trunk of her car. He had broken ribs, and his vertebrae suffered two compressed fractures; his right femur and tibia were fractured, while his left leg was even worse, the tibia obliterated. His cowboy boot ended up in the median of the highway while a quarter in his pocket was bent in half. Andre never lost consciousness. From that moment he would in part be forever defined by his injury. Critics have been eager to apply the critical lens of disability studies onto his work, but, quite frankly, this is a reductive view. Five of his six collections were published prior to his being wounded, and while his first collection of essays, *Broken Vessels* (1991), confronts the accident and his years of recovery, half of the entries were written before he was confined to his wheelchair. Elizabeth Grubgeld has made the case that "the body has always been central to the work of Andre Dubus" and that his stories written before the accident "affirm just how fragile and demanding he has always known it to be and how precisely he has understood the body, with its tyrannical needs and unscrupulous wants, to be in all of its humiliations, lovely: a site where sacraments are enacted and a boundless God enters the terrible confines of human life" ("Body, Privacy, and Community" 34). This critique is for the most part accurate. Many of the stories celebrate human strength and stamina. Graceful shapes and fair faces are found just as often as characters who lack power in their physical frames. Though his young boys often suffer from being small and clumsy and while some of his women doubt that their looks have the power to attract and hold the men they love, his mature adults have by and large moved beyond such superficial concerns.

During the long months of recovery, enduring eleven surgeries in all, Dubus was lovingly nursed by his family and friends. The impact of the car had crushed his right leg and necessitated the removal of his left leg above the knee. He would never be able to support his weight and so could not manage the prosthetic limb he had hoped would allow him to walk again. The accident caused Dubus to suffer physical pain and mental anguish for the rest of his life. In the early stages of his convalescence, his anger and frustration sometimes made him unbearable, and in 1987 his marriage to Peggy dissolved, though the two would remain connected through their complete devotion to their daughters. His love for his children and his deep Catholic faith, along with an outpouring of support from the writing community, provided him comfort during the long years of readjustment. His family's self-sacrificing response to his need, the overwhelming love and time given by his children, Pat and Peggy's many kindnesses, the generous attention and financial support offered by friends and fellow writers—all these blessings stand as testament to the redemptive power of love and forgiveness, a theme inherent in his Catholic faith and prevalent throughout his canon.

Though Dubus would struggle for almost seven years to rediscover his voice in fiction, he continued to receive awards and fellowships that added to the National Endowment for the Arts grant that he had earned in 1978; he received a second Guggenheim in 1986 as well as the Jean Stein Award and an award from the MacArthur Foundation in 1988. During his recuperation, he kept busy with his editor at Godine and published *Selected Stories* in 1988; he worked on several stories that he had in draft form. Nevertheless, the journey back to fiction writing was wearisome. In a moving tribute in *Meditations from a Moveable Chair* (1998), his second collection of essays, Dubus wrote of how he often thought of Hemingway and the way the writer had confronted his own pain, expressing beautifully the agony of mental and physical anguish. Dubus took strength from that. He was equally fortified by his daughter Nicole, who, while caring for her father, had encouraged him to let go of his worries, reassuring him that eventually he would find his way back to the short story, the genre he had mastered, the form for which he is known. She was right. He found a connection in his protagonist Robert Townsend, who, crippled by a horseback-riding accident, was struggling with the same physical and emotional demons that plagued Dubus. He learned to live alone in the wake of learning to live with daily pain and the frustrating disability that robbed him of his physical energy and temporarily stole his ability to write.

At the time he was injured, Dubus was already recognized as one of the masters of the short story and was generally compared to such other contemporary giants in the field as Raymond Carver. In her review of *Finding a Girl in America,* Julian Moynahan compared Dubus thematically to John Updike, first pointing out that though Dubus writes about middle-class and "blue-collar families" while Updike's stories are populated by the affluent, both writers are ultimately concerned with "divorce and adultery and the sorrows of children putting up with quarreling, betraying, separating parents" (12). Brian Stonehill compared Dubus to Flannery O'Connor in his review of *The Times Are Never So Bad,* not just for the more obvious southern Catholic connection but for his "ability to command our attention. Each story opens with a nearly irresistible hook. . . . The stories welcome you in, entice you skillfully" (5). This attention to craft, of the way the story is constructed, comes in part from his admiration for Anton Chekhov. He would acknowledge his debt to Chekhov and to Hemingway in many of the forty-two interviews (thirty-seven are in print while five remain on audio) that he would give over the course of his writing career.

In 1986 Dubus published a second novel, *Voices from the Moon,* while continuing to write the short stories and essays for which he is known. In a favorable review of *Finding a Girl in America,* Judith Gies pointed out that Dubus's best writing "captures the almost imperceptible erosions of daily life—the slow disintegration of marriages, the loosening of bonds between parents and children, the leaking away of self-respect. And he records the small gains—reconciliations, fresh starts, efforts to keep the machinery of our lives in working order" (42). Complications with relationships, those difficulties inherent in loving another, are at the center of his work and bind together his collections and novels. He has been celebrated for writing with "sensitivity and exactitude about ordinary people whose common lot is a narrowing of options" (Gies 42). Joyce Carol Oates and others would term this "narrowing" a form of naturalism in which characters are so limited by their circumstances that they lack choice. In a favorable review of *Separate Flights,* Oates observed that many of his characters "are trapped in stultifying marriages, though Dubus never suggests that they might have been capable of arranging other fates" (105). While this may be sparingly true, most of Dubus's protagonists, no matter how broken, struggle within their own personal ethical systems to heal themselves and those they love. For Patrick Samway, Dubus's work is "a construction site, where he structures a work of fiction, based not on reality, but on the possible that inexorably reveals the probable. Dubus gives his characters freedom; they can choose over and over again—and Dubus as author portrays forthrightly their plights" without moral judgment (Anderson 14).This struggle to harness one's possibilities and move toward a more "probable" hope can be said of Dubus's own experience as he struggled time and again to overcome and heal from the adversity in his life. In 1991 his first collection of essays, *Broken Vessels,* was a runner-up for the Pulitzer Prize. And when his short story "The Colonel's Wife" appeared in the February 1993 issue of *Playboy,* it was clear that he was back in form. The story would become part of the critically acclaimed short-story cycle *Dancing After Hours,* published in 1996.

Andre Dubus succumbed to heart failure on February 24, 1999. His last published story, "Sisters" (1999), was a reworked version of the short story "Riding North," his only attempts at the western, a genre he read and admired. The story artfully confronts two refrains from previous works, violence against women and the futility of revenge; nevertheless, the improbability of having a man singlehandedly build a coffin and dig a grave in one afternoon led his two sons, both carpenters, to tease him about the story. Dubus challenged Andre and Jeb to build his coffin when his time came and to prove him wrong by digging his grave. They did. The two men worked without rest through an evening and long into the next morning to build the simple, lovingly constructed pine box lined with his satin bed sheets by his daughter-in-law Fontaine and his first wife, Pat. Though the family and community would celebrate his life at a memorial service that winter, it was on opening day at Fenway Park, April 13, 1999, with an intimate gathering of family and close friends that Andre Dubus was buried in Haverhill at a private cemetery near the house he and Peggy had built. His sons and their devoted family friend Bill Cantwell had dug the grave the day before.

Prior to his death in 1999, Andre Dubus had developed a critical reputation as a storyteller who, in the midst of postmodern experimentation, was committed to a realistic presentation of his characters. Fellow writers such as Thomas E. Kennedy, Joyce Carol Oates, Anita Shreve, Lucy Ferriss, and Harriett Gilbert, for example, make reference to Dubus's realistic writing style. As Kennedy has concluded, Dubus's "stories fulfill Goethe's two-century old definition of the story as concerning itself with an event which might really have happened though it went unreported" ("Progress" 3). Shreve has likewise pointed out that Dubus's work "continues the American story-telling tendency toward realism that matured in the writings of F. Scott Fitzgerald and Ernest Hemingway" (136). As Judith Levine has summarized in her review of *The Times Are Never So Bad,* "Dubus's bartenders, soldiers, graduate students at small-city colleges, two-bit thieves, and security guards are burdened—and rewarded—with loyalty and love, for which they suffer, fight, betray, even kill. The narrow boundaries of their experience do not compress them emotionally or spiritually" (3). His protagonists are everyday people confronting everyday problems that have oftentimes caused catastrophic changes resulting in major shifts in perspective. The focus of the narratives is typically less on what has happened—in other words, less an emphasis on plot—than on a psychological exploration of how his various characters respond to events in their lives. Stonehill has correctly concluded that the narrative pattern of many of Dubus's stories relies on memory, "the lens that lets us look out of a single event across the whole of the life that led to it" (5). This looking back, this recounting of the events that have brought each character to his or her station in life, inevitability evokes both compassion for the struggles as well as an assurance that each human being is ultimately accountable for him or herself and loved ones. As Kennedy pointed out, "The world of Dubus's fiction is one in which the word *sin* again becomes valid, for it is a world in which men and women are responsible for their actions—and their inactions" ("Progress" 3). Broken homes, broken marriages, broken promises, broken hearts—in sum, broken people—pervade the two novels and six collections of short stories by Dubus, and his essays are oftentimes reflections of the brokenness he witnessed in his own life and in the world at large. His first published story, "The Intruder" (1963), establishes his fascination with violence and the patriarchal need to protect, a carryover, perhaps, from the southern aristocratic view of women as vulnerable, their virtue in need of defense. This struggle between innocence and desire, between loving God and breaking his commandments, is introduced in his first collection, *Separate Flights,* and is prevalent throughout his works.

His second collection of short stories, *Adultery and Other Choices* (1977), is divided into three sections: the coming-of-age stories of part 1, the military stories of part 2, and the marriage stories of part 3. These categories would serve as major themes that Dubus would take on in other works of fiction as well as in the essays he wrote. Many of the boyhood stories are set in a thinly disguised mid-1900s Lafayette, Louisiana, and feature the loosely autobiographical recurring character Paul Clement, a point Dubus would concede to many interviewers.[2] The writer's seven years in the Marine Corps would have a profound effect on his life, and while the experience helped validate his sense of manhood, his criticism of the military's homophobia and unwillingness or inability to confront the stresses of military training and combat remain central to each work. Likewise, the marriage stories condemn the repressiveness of an institution that can stifle personal expression and growth. Vivian Gornick has compared Dubus with Raymond Carver and Richard Ford and linked the three to Ernest Hemingway: "Settings vary and regional idioms intrude, but almost always it is men and women together that is being written about." She compared Hemingway's protagonists to Dubus's, who, "made inarticulate by modern life," are "vulnerable" because of "loneliness," though they "long for things to be other than they are" (1). Not all simply "long," however.

Many of the stories by Andre Dubus are written from a female perspective and take on complex themes of rejection and abuse, murder and robbery, as the various characters attempt to navigate their myriad conflicts. Likewise, the motif of domestic space appears throughout his canon and works to suggest autonomy or lack thereof. Houses become prisons or, conversely, places of refuge that reflect the protagonists' abilities to determine their course of events—or their inability to do so. The 1984 collection of novellas, *We Don't Live Here Anymore,* links the three Allison/Linhart stories that, grouped as a cycle, illustrate the protagonists' growing awareness of their spiritual isolation, metaphorically suggested by their association to home. This is precisely where Dubus's final short-story cycle, *Dancing After Hours* (1996), picks up, with the recurring characters Ted and LuAnn, who are brought together after years of empty relationships into a healthy union that celebrates the healing power of the human heart in connection with another, feelings reflected in their domestic sanctuary. As Lucy Ferriss has rightfully argued, in Dubus's fiction, "Expression of love toward another human being, whether erotic or maternal, is itself a kind of prayer or communion with the holy" (236). The satellite stories that surround the Luann and Ted stories progress along this same line, culminating in one of his most masterful works, the story of a man, crippled by an unfortunate accident, who has refused to withdraw from life. His example gives the protagonist the courage to let go of her own fear and to trust in love again. As Kennedy artfully concluded, "The hunger of Dubus's characters to transcend the solitude bounded by their flesh is where their progress toward the communion of love begins" ("Progress" 4).

Woven through Dubus's work as well is the importance of faith, the mysterious draw and healing power of the unconditional bond between parent and child demonstrated through the abiding example of God's love for his son and his son's sacrifice for the world's sins. At the other end of the spectrum are the few stories of men and women who, in their despair, have no sense of peace, who feel trapped by their lives and victimized by their circumstance. Most of his stories fall somewhere between these divergent extremes and focus on the importance of ritual, a theme that again links Dubus to Hemingway. Rituals dominate Dubus's stories, a carryover from his Catholic upbringing, while at the center of his works is an emphasis on moral responsibility demonstrated through an established code of behavior oftentimes constructed as a way to confront guilt and remorse. For Mark Osteen, the rituals take "a peculiar form": "Again and again Dubus's characters recoil from or reflect upon a traumatic experience and then engage in a rite of reenactment through which they hope to convert the experience and gain control over it" (74). In this, Osteen was correct. Many of the stories focus on this metaphorical necessity to find the way back home. Secular patterns of behavior as well as rituals of religion help the fallible learn to live with the mistakes they have made, acts of betrayal against themselves and those they love.

In all of Dubus's fiction, characters are limited or motivated by their respective surroundings. Dubus would admit in an interview with this author, "We are all shaped by our environment. I don't get beyond that. Within that, we are morally responsible" (238). In the final analysis, his protagonists are a mixture of those lost in their own misfortunes and those who make peace and move on. These same themes dominate his essays as well, a genre to which he turned exclusively in the years following his accident. These personal essays, collected in *Broken Vessels* and *Meditations from a Moveable Chair,* offer glimpses into the author's point of view on topics ranging from his belief in ghosts to his faith in God, and his first-person narratives suggest that, like his characters, Dubus himself oftentimes felt limited by his environment and his biology at the same time that he celebrated his ability to choose how he responded to these limitations. As Frederick Busch would write for Donald Anderson's collection *Andre Dubus: Tributes,* published two years after Dubus's death, the novels, the short-story collections, and the two volumes of essays ultimately reflect "the soul in its agonies and occasional triumphs" (41). So, too, did Dubus's life.

CHAPTER 2

Boyhood and Military Life

To understand the writings of Andre Dubus is first to recognize the overwhelming influence of the region into which he was born. Dubus was both Catholic and southern, the only son and youngest child of a father to whom he felt he never measured up. What it meant to be a man, what it meant to assimilate with his peers and to feel confident in himself in spite of his small frame, his lack of athletic ability, and his perceptive intelligence at odds with the deep class and racial divides—these issues dominate the short stories of the man who eventually joined the U.S. Marine Corps to prove to his father that he was worthy of respect. As David Godine, his publisher for the majority of his writing career, would sum up in a conversation in April 2015 with this author, to understand the works of Andre Dubus is to understand the formidable influence of both the Catholic Church and the marines on the mind of the artist. The importance of his faith and his sometimes overwhelming insecurity and self-doubt are best understood through the stories of his southern boyhood that surface throughout his collections.

In 1963 Dubus published his first story, "The Intruder" (included in *Dancing After Hours*), which introduces major themes that run throughout his canon. For that reason, a lengthy discussion of the story is essential. Kenneth Girard is a young boy who struggles to live up to the fantasy roles he plays in the woods that surround his parents' summer retreat at the lake outside of Lafayette, Louisiana. The youngest child and only son spends the hot afternoons living out his dreams of being like the heroic cowboys and soldiers who entertain him in the Saturday matinee movies he watches during the school year or on the late-show television of summertime, and because of this, he "liked being alone" (5). Free to use his imagination and create for himself each scenario of success, Kenneth would save "a beautiful girl" (3), shoot down outlaws in a western town, hit the winning run "so far and high that the outfielders did not even move," or lead his men bravely into battle (4). Within these four examples of heroism lie the conflicts of Dubus's boy protagonists who would all be too young for World War II. Several would be too clumsy to succeed in sports. All would be sensitive to the feelings of others, never treating girls as objects of conquest. In portraying each boy—from Kenneth to Paul Clement, who makes an appearance in four of the stories from *Adultery and Other Choices* and then reappears in "Goodbye" in *The Times Are Never So Bad* (1983), and from Richie Stowe of Dubus's second novel, *Voices from the Moon* (1984), to Gerry Fontenot, a more mature version of all three—Dubus's fiction is preoccupied with the notion of what it means to be male during the last few decades before television coverage of the Vietnam war and the volatile issues of civil rights would rewrite and restructure everything for everyone, Andre Dubus included. Likewise, having lived in southwest Louisiana and grown up Catholic in an area heavily influenced by the church, Dubus would reference the influence his faith had on his fiction in almost every interview he gave. As he would tell John Smolens in 1994, "My Catholicism . . . is always there, whether it's evident or not" (Edenfield 212), and whether religion is central to his boy protagonists or not, each is influenced by the Catholic Church, for better or worse.

Kenneth's older sister is everything the boy believes he is not, popular in school and at ease with herself, confident in her beauty. Though he is never in conflict with his father, who is absent from the family because of his weekday job obligations, and though he loves his mother, who nourishes him and gives him the freedom of time alone, his beautiful sister, Connie, "is the only person with whom, for his entire life, he had been nearly perfectly at ease" (5). With her, he does not have to pretend to be the hero he fears he is not: "He could be silent with her or he could say whatever occurred to him and he never had to think about it first to assure himself that it was not foolish or, worse, uninteresting" (5). Only with Connie can the boy who struggles to understand himself actually be himself. Connected to her by their very makeup, the color of their hair and skin, Kenneth feels a kinship that gives him hope that he will one day mature to be the type of man his father has become, strong and successful and loved by a wife who happily tends a tidy and happy home, a reflection of their family. Yet only hoping, lacking confidence, he measures himself against what he knows to be untrue: "He believed that Connie thought he was exactly like her, that he was talkative and well liked. But she never saw him with his classmates. He felt that he was deceiving her" (5). It is this deception that makes him even more vigilant than he might be in his determination to protect his sister from harm and to keep her close.

Connie makes two statements, the first to her brother and the second to her parents, that foreshadow the events to come. When Kenneth returns from the woods with his .22 rifle, she asks if he has killed anything. When her parents ready themselves to leave the two alone for the evening to drive into the city for a party, she assures her mother that she and Kenneth will go to bed early so they will be able to attend mass the next day. She does retire early but not to sleep. Instead, she clears the way for her boyfriend to sneak into her bedroom once Kenneth has gone to bed. And while Kenneth has not managed or even attempted to shoot anything in the woods, he is successful in killing Connie's suitor, whom he murders in misguided defense.

Protection of women is a recurring pattern in the first four collections of stories. "The Intruder" was not collected until 1996, in his last short-story cycle, *Dancing After Hours.* Interestingly enough, it is this collection that focuses on a woman, LuAnn Briggs, who learns to defend herself instead of relying on any male companion to define or protect her. She rises out of a complicated understanding of herself to defeat the intruders who attempt to take away the life that she has carefully built with her husband and equal partner, Ted. Her development is intensified by the short-story cycle's opening with the story of a young boy who ruins his life, destroys his sister's happiness, and shatters his family's peace. Kenneth resorts to violence in an inherent need to protect the virtue of his virginal sister, the only image of Connie with which he is comfortable.

On the night that the shooting occurs, Kenneth has to make adjustments in the way he sees his sister. After their parents leave for town, he catches her smoking. She brings him into a deeper confidence by making him promise to keep the secret from her father, and though he goes along with it, he "could not watch her" and pretends to read a book, resorting to an activity that usually brings him solitary peace. Yet watching her with her cigarette, he understands that "she had been smoking for a long time . . . without his knowing it. He was hurt. He laid down the book" (8) and escapes outside, where he falls into a fantasy in which he overpowers a guard, shoots a general, and secures papers vital to the war effort. The military exploits provide Kenneth with a confident image of himself that matches the way he wants to be perceived by his father, a boyish need for approval reappearing in subsequent Dubus stories. Always the hero in his daydreams, Kenneth is at ease with the violence he has conditioned himself to believe is necessary in defense of what he honors. In his fantasies and in fact, he has mastered the art of shooting, for his marksmanship is his one talent, the skill that he perfects alone during his long days in the woods. His sees his cleverness with books as simply another embarrassment that sets him at odds with his ideal of a southern boy in post–World War II America.

Though most happy alone, Kenneth is comfortable with Connie's girlfriends, who all admire his looks and give him attention, and with these girls he "tries to be witty and usually was" (11). He is even at ease with certain boys in her group who lack the perceived swagger that comes from being successful at team sports. He is intimidated only by the confident young men and by the athletic boys whose ease paralyzes Kenneth's "tongue and even his mind" (10). With these visitors, these "intruders" in his home who violate his image of himself as worthy of his sister's affection, he grows silent and from the sidelines simply watches. Douglass is no exception. Into this very day of change in his perception of his sister, Kenneth notes Douglass's muscular build with which he cannot compete. Shy and anxious, he cleans his gun to impress his sister's boyfriend, who, taking the .22 in hand demonstrates his own ease with a rifle, aiming and pulling the trigger, which he compliments, before sending Connie to get him a beer. In a bit of domestic roleplaying, she waits on him, cooking for him and later smoking on the couch, where the two sit together while Kenneth, like a child, watches television alone. The tension between the young boy and the suitor to whom he compares himself will reemerge in future stories by Dubus in which sensitive, shy, perceptive boys on the edge of sexual awakening seek refuge in the company of flattering girls, sometimes sisters, with whom they do not have to compete. Within the comforting circle of female companionship, heightened by an awareness of their own bodies' emerging desires, these young boys are able, if only temporarily, to find their place.

Like the sentinel he feels he must be, he guards his sister once Douglass leaves, watching from his bedroom that "extended forward from the rest of the house, so that, from his bed, he could look through the window to his left and see the living room and Connie's bedroom" (15). The living room he views as his family's retreat from the world: Connie's bedroom her virginal chamber and Kenneth her protector, charged and entrusted by his father. Conflicted by his lust over a picture in a magazine of a female whose breasts and exposed stomach make him feel guilty enough to turn to his rosary, he exercises a bit, feeling the biceps that he hopes are strengthening, before slipping into bed, where he prays and watches over his home. When the boy sees what he learns too late is Douglass's shadowy form outside his sister's window, he methodically loads his gun while imagining "a large, bearded man" (16); Kenneth's every movement here is as precise and calculated as those he has perfected during his summer afternoon daydreams in the woods. When the "prowler" (17) touches his sister's screen, a metaphorical hymen the potential rapist threatens to penetrate, Kenneth aims at the head, and the screams that follow are not those of a young girl terrified by an intruder, but of one who has been violated and betrayed, not by her would-be lover but by her own brother's vigilance. Screaming her boyfriend's name, she pushes Kenneth away.

It is never clear whether or not the boy knows, even subconsciously, that the intruder was Douglass. He never admits to himself or his parents whether his true perception is simply blocked by his easy shift into fantasy or whether he uses this escape into roleplaying to justify his retaliation at his anger over his alternate vision of his sister. Perhaps Douglass's death is simply a mistake. The lie his father tells him as he comforts his distraught son sets up the same falsehoods to which parents seeking to protect their children will resort. The lack of resolution is as comfortless as the impossible promise Kenneth makes to himself, though it seems to be the desire of most of Dubus's fiction: to "throw all guns and cruelty and sex and tears into the sea" (19). Many of the complicated patterns that dominate Dubus's fiction are at play in this first published work.

Kenneth's confusion about sex and his desire to protect his sister stem in part from the influence of the Catholic Church on many boys growing up in southwest Louisiana, and "If They Knew Yvonne," collected in *Separate Flights* (1975), confronts the Church's teachings head on. The first-person narrative, dedicated to Dubus's sons, Andre and Jeb, begins with a central fact: "I grew up in Louisiana, and for twelve years I went to a boys' school taught by Christian Brothers, a Catholic religious order" (99). The protagonist, Harry Dugal, also attends Catholic school and is educated by the Christian Brothers. The similarities do not end there. Like Dubus's parents, Harry's mother is Catholic while his father is Episcopalian; secondly, the boy is close to and influenced by his older sister. The story is so close to home, in fact, that Gene Lyons, in his favorable review of *Separate Flights,* concludes that the story reads more like a memoir than a work of fiction (249). Perhaps having two religions in the home gives Harry the courage to question his church's teachings on masturbation, but not before he is so guilt ridden by his inability to stop that he considers self-mutilation. After being denied absolution, the young man seeks out a different priest, for he is not "the renegade" his divorced sister is—"I wanted absolution" (118)—and Father Grassi, thankfully, provides a balance to "poor Father Broussard," who would agree, perhaps, with the book Grassi burned when he left seminary, a book of "moral theology" that stated that "masturbation was worse than rape, because at least rape was the carrying out of a natural instinct" (119). This statement neither the young priest nor his confessor can support. When the two talk frankly about sin and sex, what Harry concludes is that his true sin is having bedded a girl he does not love, though the two had long been sweethearts. Rather than punish him, Father Grassi tells him, "for your penance, say alleluia three times" (120).

The celebration is tied to the protagonist's revelation that though the body and its desires are complicated, betraying another's love demands contrition. As Thomas A. Wendorf has rightfully asserted, "Harry discovers that sexual morality involves not only his own soul but also the souls of others, and that it is in the flesh and blood that he must learn that wisdom" (135). As if he were anticipating much of Dubus's fiction yet to come, Lyons added to this: "No amount of masculine or feminist posturing has been able to conceal or change" that "casual copulation seems to make almost everybody sad" (248). Confessing his rejection of Yvonne, Harry is at last free to let go of his guilt. In the final scene, crabbing with his young nephews, he watches the boys tell "each crab goodbye," and he is moved by their "strong little bodies, those kind hearts" (121). The binding image of body and heart brings the story to the right conclusion: a celebration of love and its complex responsibilities, a theme that not only ties together the collection but the entire canon. As James N. Baker stated in his positive review of *Adultery and Other Choices,* "The people [Dubus] writes about—children, adolescents, adults—wrestle with universal fears: of parents, of love, of self-destruction. The protagonists usually win out, sometimes impermanent, sometimes for good. That Dubus can repeatedly persuade us that this is possible is the marvel of his art" (100).

Paul Clement, who appears in four of the five stories from part 1 of *Adultery and Other Choices* (1977), likewise grows up in a small southern town, heavily influenced by the Catholic bayou country of Louisiana. Like the writer, Paul has two older sisters to whom he feels close and a mother who is overprotective in her desire to shelter her only son from what she and Paul are convinced is his father's disapproval. This alliance simply deepens the divide and further complicates the father-son relationship. Just as Kenneth does, Paul temporarily escapes his own shyness and insecurity by both daydreaming and praying for a stronger, more athletic body. Paul daydreams of a girl who was his best friend back in Baton Rouge before his father's job transfer relocated the family to Lafayette at the end of his second school year. Stronger and more confident than Paul, Marshall—even her name works counter to the femininity she resisted—was his champion, defending him against schoolyard bullies. In his present-day fantasies, however, she is transformed into a graceful, developed young woman of sixteen who, wearing a white dress like a virginal bride, embraces Paul's future self, "handsome and bigger and stronger, too, because he had been praying every night and at Mass for God to make him an athlete" (1).[1] Though his mother and sisters had known about Marshall, he had never confided to his father that he had such a girlfriend, ashamed, perhaps, that she was fearless while Paul resisted both her kisses and her desires to play hard, to send them all the way around and over the top as she pumped the swing the two shared at a friend's party. His mother urges him to open up to his father, who just "doesn't know how to talk to children," though he loves his son, she explains (2). However, Paul is as tentative with the man as he is with Marshall, whom he agrees to kiss only if she closes her eyes, while the "boy who was It passed by without looking in" (2). The "It" boy, like the popular and athletic boys whom Paul is too shy to befriend, never really sees him, and Paul's missing the game while he and Marshall hide together in the garage, sitting on the running board of a car, foreshadows what is to come in "Goodbye," collected in *The Times Are Never So Bad* (1983). Feeling finally worthy of his father's pride, Paul will eventually escape the inadequacy he feels by packing the car and heading out of town with his new wife to begin his service in the Marine Corps.

Until that time, though, the four stories in *Adultery* record the ever-growing distance between the male members of the Clement family. Paul knows he is "supposed to" enjoy spending time with his father, that as a boy he should want to be on the golf course with the men his father plays with on Sundays, earning money by serving as his dad's caddie; instead, he dreads each outing and sits "stiffly, looking through the windshield" (4). Though he earns his father's compliments for his day's work on the golf course, the two do not engage, and Paul walks behind him, embarrassed by the golf cart he pulls while the other boys, permanent caddies, carry their golfers' bags over their broad shoulders. In the clubhouse afterwards, Paul watches his father drink beer and converse with a woman whom he realizes is very different from his mother and who, like Marshall, enjoyed the company of males and was comfortable smoking and drinking, swearing and laughing, while Paul's father talked with her about golf. In this comparison Paul feels guilty, not for witnessing the companionship that his mother is missing, but for somehow "betraying his father, as though he were his mother's spy, recording every time his father said 'Betsy.' He decided to count the beers his father drank, so if his mother said something Paul could defend him" (7). He is conflicted in the love he feels for his mother and his need for the masculine camaraderie that he desires with his "old man," who speaks with a new "quality that was almost tenderness, almost affection." Yet, he lets down both himself and his father with his lack of enthusiasm: "it was as if his soul wanted to talk and hug his father but his body could not, and all he could do was in silence love his father as though he were a memory, as the afternoon already was a memory" (8).

The son's inability to express himself to his father is exacerbated in the second of the Paul Clement stories, "Contrition," and the divide is accentuated by his friend's easy connection with his own father. Frances Taliaferro's favorable review of *Adultery and Other Choices,* which it compares to a Hopper landscape, a "world of quiet melodies," finds "Contrition" the best of the bunch as it "says all that ever need be said about the pain of family love" (87). When Paul compares his friend Eddie Kirkpatrick's family to his own, he recognizes that each member of his household is isolated one from the other. The Kirkpatricks, on the other hand, share everything, including the knowledge that Eddie is unhappy at school because of the same bullying and feelings of inadequacy that Paul wordlessly suffers. While Eddie's discontentedness ends when he reaches the sanctuary of home, Paul's is intensified by his understanding that "children should be seen and not heard and at times it seemed that Paul's silence made him invisible too and he could listen like a spy" and make discoveries about his family. When he compares his father's quiet and imperfect strength to the kindness of Mr. Kirkpatrick, Paul pretends to believe his own lie: "*Mine's better*" (13). The divide between the son and his father makes him tentative about all men, all fathers, and he longs to destroy the ease he witnesses in the Kirkpatrick household to make his own unease more bearable. Conflicted, he feels drawn toward Mr. Kirkpatrick, "drawn to him as though by trust and love," which leads to guilt and shame for his feelings of fear in relation to his own father (14).

When Paul decides to play an instrument like his friend, he and Eddie take up the French horn in spite of their original plan to play trumpet, banking on the promise from Brother Eugene that the boys would be able to play in the school band much sooner. His inability to speak frankly to Brother Eugene, to tell him that he wants to play the trumpet instead, mirrors his inability to voice his feelings to his father. Though he can articulate what he wants to his mother and can temporarily share his sisters' enthusiasm over his new adventure, with his father he remains silent, afraid to express anything that turns the paternal gaze on him, eyes that remind him of "the relief he felt at all his father's departures and the fear at his arrivals" (16). Rather than speak honestly to anyone, he daydreams, longing to be away from home on an island of women who care for him.

When he fails, for he only pretends to practice, his shame is furthered by the knowledge that his father has spent money on a new horn rather than renting an old one as Eddie's father has done. To prove that he can afford it, his father spends one hundred dollars on a lovely instrument that Paul will never master, its beauty further proof to the boy of his own unworthiness. When his mother later comes to his defense, the divide between father and son is deepened. What she calls sensitivity, though, is for the father further evidence of his son's cowardly nature, which is confirmed by Brother Eugene's lack of respect for a boy who quits so easily, a boy he believes has no "pride" (20). Ironically, the issue of pride is more related to Paul's parents and Brother Eugene, who each use the boy in his or her own way. Brother Eugene wants to be respected in his profession by leading a school band improved by two French horn players; Paul's father proves his financial security by purchasing an expensive instrument that his son will show off in lessons; Paul's mother uses her better understanding and ease with her son as a judgment against her spouse's coarse nature and then uses her husband's confusion at his inability to please his son and wife to punish him for his drinking, his temper, and his time away from home. Paul takes in an impression of himself that at ten years of age he is ill-equipped to reshape or redefine, not even under his kind sister's words of comfort. Instead, he "silently asked his father's question—*What's he good for?*—and he could not accept the answer of [his sister's] gaze and touch." He feels weakened by his mother's fear for him, her perception of him as a "little boy," and in spite of his island fantasies, he longs for a different, stronger self that never has to be protected by women as he is in his own family, a self like his father rather than the sensitive boy he fears he will always be (22). He combats what he sees as a sin of weakness by refusing comfort, sacrificing himself in defense of his father, seeking "contrition" in order to be worthy of his father's pride and ultimately his love.

To prove that he can and will be more than this sweet boy his mother and sisters love, he becomes the tormenter he both fears and respects in the final story of the trilogy, "The Bully." Paul takes out his anger on a helpless kitten whose inexperience with cruelty makes it an easy victim that neither fights back nor runs away. He punishes the weakness of the defenseless animal as a way to punish himself, a warped form of contrition that has little power to comfort just as his cruelty to the trusting and helpless being only enhances his self-loathing. He comes to admire a new boy at school who is strong and friendly and unafraid, whose powerful body can take the blows as well as he gives them in the afternoon boxing matches at their school. He admires Roland as he admires the cowboys in the Saturday movies he watches with his friend Eddie, who, like Paul, lives with a "body in a world of running, pushing, yelling boys" (28). This world, for Paul, tells him every day that he is unlovable, that only women who make excuses for him will love him, rendering him powerless to withstand Larry, the schoolyard bully, who ultimately drowns in the bayou. Larry is swept away in a muddy current more powerful than his meanness, which had served to hide the shame he felt at his poverty and lack of intellect. Paul's movement toward grace and a new sense of himself in the world come when he is able to pray for Larry's soul, which Paul believes is suffering in purgatory, "where souls thrashed in pain but their faces gazed with the serenity of hope" (32). In praying for Larry, Paul prays for himself, absolving himself of sin as he prepares to enter his father's world of men.

This he does in "Cadence," the first story of part 2 in *Adultery and Other Choices,* when Paul joins the Marine Corps. The story opens with Paul standing in the summer twilight, the time of day metaphorically suggesting his movement into the temporary dark thoughts of self-doubt that almost defeat him, his fear of failure "nearly unbearable." It is, in fact, "physical: it took a penetrating fall into his legs and weakened his knees so that he felt he was not supported by muscle and bone but by faint nerves alone" (63). As he suffers through the evening run, he dreams of going home, of some power outside himself that would deliver him without shame back to Louisiana in some "magical or lucky way" (64). He runs through the darkness, remembering, flashing back to his first day at Quantico when he arrived in his ROTC uniform rather than the civilian clothes worn by the other recruits. His uniform ironically betrays him as the khaki that he hoped would signify him as part of a unit conversely makes him visible and, consequently, a target for his drill sergeant's temper.

Initially, his body betrays him, first by being healthy enough to pass the medical exam but too weak to endure the demands of basic training without constant physical suffering and self-doubt. Now, however, the action of the story takes place during the daylight hours, at the breakfast table where Paul eats large meals, hoping to add weight to his small frame. The obstacle course becomes symbolic of all that he must overcome, not simply the strenuous demands of pushups and trail runs, but his tendency to befriend other boys like himself who lack physical strength. When he defeats Hugh on the athletic field by finding his "balance," using his center as a way to win, he makes the first step toward becoming the man he believes his father would respect. Though Paul comes to Quantico having already graduated from college, he still sees himself as a boy, not part of the male world dominated by men like his father and the gunnery sergeant Hathaway. It is a fraternity to which he has longed to belong since his first summer job in Louisiana, when, at sixteen, he helped dig a foundation under the watchful eye of a supervisor told by Paul's father to "make a man of him" (78). The flashback comes with the taste of the salt tablets Hathaway advises after Paul successfully runs the grinder in spite of the fact that he throws up and lags behind the rest, coming in last but not quitting as Hugh, another recruit, does. His very skin color has separated him from the "Negroes, digging a trench for the foundation" (78), another metaphorical reference to his working to find his base strength. In earlier stories, when he was a child, Paul had been protected by females in both fantasy and in the everyday realities of his life. Remembering that summer day, Paul thinks of his father, who came not to rescue him but to bring him a hat so that his son could withstand the summer heat.

Dubus would return to this experience in his essay "Digging," from his collection *Meditations from a Moveable Chair,* which recounts the story of his first summer job in great detail. Like the protagonist Paul, Dubus was small-framed and lightweight, a scant 105 pounds at age sixteen. The essay follows the same narrative structure as many of his stories do, opening with the action in present time, then flashing back to those moments in the past that build toward the main conflict. Dubus, like Paul, was "shy" with his father and sought refuge in his imagination. Under that hot July sun, Dubus, like Paul, helped grown men dig a foundation, eventually finding the strength to complete the job he was at first convinced would defeat him, until one day "the foundation was done. . . . it was part of me" (31). As he did in that memory of long ago, Paul in a sense regurgitates his inner doubt, ridding himself of the food he consistently identifies with his mother, vomiting out all pampering weaknesses, his first transference from past feminine safe havens to the long and difficult roads navigated by men. By strengthening his body, he strengthens his self-image, pushing through the heat and pain and fatigue into a "certainty" that "descended on him warmly, like the morning sun" (83). He is symbolically reborn into a new Paul Clement, no longer isolated, but part of a unit sure to make his father and, consequently, himself proud as he joins the rank of men.

As with all of the boy protagonists in Dubus's stories who are troubled by the small frames and strong intellects that divide them from the herd of boys with whom they long to identify, peace and certainty come from the longed for and finally attained bodily strength and determination exhibited by each of their fathers. The military gives Paul the rituals necessary to harness his courage and to feel worthy of paternal love. Unlike Munson, who quits and is cut off and shunned like the cowardly elephant in the allegory told by their drill sergeant, Paul finds his rightful place as he "dissolve[s] into unity with the rest of the platoon" (82). Ironically, by losing himself in the group, he finds his inner strength and potential, which come to fruition in the final Paul Clement story, "Goodbye," collected in *The Times Are Never So Bad* (1983). Married now and having successfully completed basic training, Paul and his father meet as equals as Paul's more mature point of view is able to take in his parents' failings: their troubled marriage and their lack of intimacy, his father's insecurities and his inability to articulate his love for his son, his mother's lack of respect for her husband's career and her unspoken shame that her marriage has brought her down in the world. As her husband had previously done to his son by purchasing a new French horn that he could not really afford, making Paul's failure at mastering the instrument that much harder for the boy to bear, Paul's mother sets impossible standards for her son's farewell dinner, guaranteeing disaster. The father cannot measure up to the man his wife expects him to be just as the son has felt, until this final evening at home, that he, likewise, will always fail her. But with his beautiful bride, their marriage hastened by their expected child, Paul stands separate from his parents in his own union with Judith. The two are ready for a new life on a different coast, where Paul will be able to decide for himself what sort of man he is meant to be.

That Paul's marriage will more than likely experience casualties as damaging as his parents' is suggested by his willingness to risk his wife and unborn child's safety. Paul allows his drunk father to drive Judith home from the country club after the two are sent by his mother to collect his father from his card game. Earlier, Paul had sat at the head of the table while the elder Clement had refused to come home to the farewell dinner his wife had meticulously planned. Yet his mother's attempt to replace her husband with her grown and outwardly respectful son is undercut by Paul's having transferred his sense of loyalty from his mother to his father, sympathizing with the man's inability to measure up to her expectations. Overhearing his mother's voice on the phone, "hurt, bitter, whining," he confirms that his loyalty resides with his father, who "by their natures were bound to keep sober women waiting at their stoves" (74). Even Paul is uncertain whether he believes this or is simply acting out a part that more closely identifies him with his idea of a man. What he thinks, nevertheless, is "though his mother was right, his father wrong . . . he was against her" (75). Though he has been to college and survived basic training, he still lacks the perspective necessary to break the pattern of expecting too much, as his mother does, and giving too little, as his father has always done. The final scene in the country club parking lot foreshadows the young couple's future. He risks his new family to keep his father from a lonely ride home, in spite of Judith's turning her eyes to her husband, "looking up" at him (80). Paul lacks the courage to name the selfishness that is at the core of his father's actions, a selfishness that comes to haunt and oftentimes destroy the marriages in Dubus's works. All Paul can do is ask what went wrong; yet the father has no counsel for his son.

This is the theme of the second of Dubus's novels, *Voices from the Moon* (1984). Like Paul Clement, twelve-year-old Richie Stowe is a Catholic boy who is deeply affected by his parents' marital troubles. Sensitive and smart like Paul, Richie is aware of but tentative about girls and their mysterious power. Yet Richie's similarities to Paul depart here to follow deeper roads of sorrow over the breakup of his parents, which he believes in his profoundly religious heart to go against the Catholic Church he hopes one day to serve. His waking days are defined by his parents' failure to stay together, and he suffers, feeling "the opening of wounds he had believed were healed, felt again the deep and helpless sorrow, and the anger too because he . . . had done nothing at all to cause it" (4). Further betrayal comes to the family when his father and his brother's ex-wife fall in love and plan to marry, hoping to exorcise the demons of their ruined relationships. In this decision, Richie stands to lose not only the security of a two-parent family but his brother as well, who at first cannot reconcile himself to having his ex-wife as his step-mother. These complicated relationships, justified by love over which the adults claim little control, are found in other works by Dubus. Responsible men and women who run successful businesses, who manage the daily workings of their lives outside of the home, forfeit their will and claim not to choose but to surrender to something over which they have no power. In his explanation to his oldest son, attempting to justify his love for Brenda, Greg claims that his midlife recognition of time being wasted came from his deep awareness that her love, "like a completion of who you are," made him aware that he must act whether he wanted to or not, that he must fill the "holes" dug into his life (34). Yet, in his admitted weakness, he begins to fear that even this woman "would become a duty. Because when you fought so much and so hard, against pain like this as well as the knee-deep bullshit of the world, so you could be free to lie in the shade of contentment and love, the great risk was that you would be left without joy or passion, and in the long evenings of respite and solitude would turn to the woman you loved with only the distracted touch, the distant murmurs of tired responsibility" (36). His use of the word *responsibility* transforms these obligations of love into a sort of curse. Set against his youngest son's true understanding of the joy of commitment, Greg appears shallow, the justification of his behavior both trite and suspect: "Will is for those bullshit guys to write books about" (7), he concludes, a reminder, perhaps, that asserting one's will in the face of temptation is one of Dubus's consistent themes.

Adults behaving badly in the name of love and justifying their behavior as beyond their control, using their selfish needs to feel complete rather than reaffirming their commitments to their families may be found in Dubus's earliest stories, in particular the Hank and Edith Allison/Jack and Terry Linhart trilogy, which spans three of his collections: "We Don't Live Here Anymore" from *Separate Flights* (1975), "Adultery" from *Adultery and Other Choices* (1977), and the title story from *Finding a Girl in America* (1980). As the stories progress, so do the characters, who mature into a better understanding of responsibility, letting go of their self-involvement, which is finally replaced by a more mature level of commitment to their families and, ultimately, their beliefs in something deeper and more spiritually satisfying than physical desire. Interestingly, in a nod, perhaps, to the romantic notion of the child serving as a guide for the father, Richie Stowe has a better understanding of love than either of his parents will ever possess.

The pain that the boy suffers over his parents' divorce, compounded by his father's betrayal of his oldest son and his mother's decision to seal herself away from her former family, is soothed by his daily communion with God in prayer and in the receiving of the sacrament. Rising early in the summer months following his father's confession of his love for his former daughter-in-law, Richie pedals his bicycle under the "long arch of green branches of trees," the streets of his New England town an extension of the Catholic Church toward which he rides: "As he pedaled and shifted gears he prayed for his anger to leave him." When he arrives at the sanctuary, he prays again: "Please Jesus Christ Our Lord help me, then said to Him: It will be very hard to be a Catholic in our house." Richie understands that the church views his parents as sinners, yet his love for them makes it hard for him to reconcile his Catholic beliefs to this view of a mother who he knows loves him in spite of her need to isolate herself. Likewise, he knows his father is devoted to him in spite of his lack of will, "knowing it would be hard not only in the today and tomorrow of twelve years old, but even harder as he grew older and had to face the temptations that everyone in the family had succumbed to" (5). To combat what he fears is an inevitable slide into a secular world that lacks the moral touchstones of his faith, Richie contemplates giving his life to the Catholic Church, where the sacrament of communion makes him feel "that he embraced the universe, and was in the arms of God" (10). He shares his concerns with the young Father Oberti, who helps him see his family not as sinners but as those who are motivated by love, as "people who love each other, and as painful as it is for others, and even if it *is* wrong, it's still love, and that is always near the grace of God" (12). Though he accepts the young boy's view, which he acknowledges and even affirms, he challenges Richie to see beyond his current perceptions. The young priest helps him move past condemnation into an acceptance of the best of what his family has to offer, shedding his anger as he takes in the wide parameters of love that the boy is only coming to understand.

In this moment of grace, he moves from the church altar, where he had received the sacrament of communion, into another ritual, another sacrament that, though secular, is elevated to the spiritual. In interviews Dubus spoke about the sacraments of daily actions that, motivated by love, transform the mundane into the sacred, that "a really harmonious person can be walking through the supermarket, picking up a head of lettuce for the family, and be absolutely fulfilled and peaceful in the realization of the moment that this is an eternal sacrament . . . that this is the feeding of flesh that has gone on and on and on forever. And it's not an errand anymore. The clock isn't running anymore. This is very precious" (Edenfield 166). This awareness is best illustrated in "Out of the Snow," the final LuAnne and Ted Briggs story in *Dancing*

After Hours (1996). Yet this important viewpoint appears in his early works as well, in particular the second of the Edith Allison stories, "Adultery." Both works will be discussed in detail in subsequent chapters. Here, however, it is important to point out the metaphorical implications of Richie's walking into his father's home just as he has left his Father's sanctuary, where at the altar he received the body and blood of Christ and where he will now break his fast at his father's table, receiving the pancakes and eggs, the bacon and juice, immediately following his prayer: "*Please Jesus Christ Our Lord help us,* as he went up the stairs into the kitchen" (39). In the quiet of that morning ritual, Ritchie receives a spiritual understanding that helps him recover from anger and judgment as he recognizes a truth that he puts into action in the final moments of the novel. In this new awareness prompted by the young priest's wise counsel, Richie expands his understanding of love by blending the two faiths of his fathers, the one secular and the other holy, but not separate, instead united, an echo of the transcendental metaphor of the arch of green tree branches. As he cooks, the father looks his son in the eyes while speaking of love and loneliness. In his young son's forgiveness, just as he has obtained his older son's forgiveness the night before, Greg no longer appears selfish and sinful, but as simply a man following "nature's way . . . and come to think of it natural must come from the word nature, and the needs that Mother Nature put in people, or God, of course, God" (40). The setting, the kitchen filled with the ritual acts of preparing food for the nourishment of his son, provides the transference and sets up the conclusion of the novel as Richie lets go of his anger, lets go of his compartmentalized view of the world, defined and, in fact, limited by a narrow, censored understanding of love. This transference is possible only because of Father Oberti, who opens Richie to a less limited perspective of love, demonstrated by his father's acts of love to him and the seed of understanding that blooms in the final scene: that God is present in all things, in a young girl's kiss, in the arching green branches of trees, in the pancakes his father serves, in the night stars. This opening up to the riches of life, suggested by his very name, is illuminated by the contrasting self-involvement of the adults in his family. The boy stands as testament to the possibilities of living a moral life in the secular world: that grace comes in the daily acts of living just as it does in receiving the holy sacraments. To understand Andre Dubus's fiction is to understand this view of the world as it is demonstrated throughout his canon.

The final section of the novel, which begins and ends in Richie's point of view, reaches closure on the young boy's struggle to remain true to his faith, which might include his one day joining the priesthood, while at the same time purely opening himself to the possibilities of desire. His attraction to Melissa, a girl more experienced than he, has made him acutely aware of the physical.

Knowing that she will be out with her dog for its evening run, he rides his bike to the baseball field, set against dark woods, where she sits in the grass, smoking a cigarette. Her quick kiss earlier that day has lingered in his memory, but he is drawn to her as much for her conversation as for anything else. Sitting next to her on the grass, he is aware of his body, and when she takes his arm, he flexes his muscle, notices her knee touching his. John Updike, in his review of the novel, unfortunately, misinterpreted Melissa's intentions and her place in Richie's growing awareness of the variant possibilities for love. Updike saw her as "one of the youngest temptresses in fiction" and blamed her for Richie's decision not to become a priest (94). This is a narrow and condemning view of a girl who, instead of corrupting Richie, helps him come to the realization that engaging in the world and connecting with others is simply another way to serve God.[2]

In fact, turning to the church in some vain attempt to escape sin is not the answer. Richie has to learn to live in the world with all of its flaws, with all of its less than perfect human beings who are still deserving of love, an understanding to which many of Dubus's characters must come. Here, Richie's sexual awakening is purified by the night, the grass, and the stars—all connected to the earlier justification by his father that what is natural comes from nature, which ultimately comes from God. In this moment, he is free to share his pain with another and is further released from his anger at his parents and the fear he has for his family by his newly found connection with Melissa: "He felt Melissa's hand in his, and the beating of his heart she both quickened and soothed, and he smelled the length of her beside him, and heard in the trees the song of cicadas like the distant ringing of a thousand tambourines. He saw in the stars the eyes of God too, and was grateful for them, as he was for the night and the girl he loved. He lay on the grass and the soft summer earth, holding Melissa's hand, and talking to the stars" (126). Her body and voice combine with the earth and with the eyes of God, and he speaks to God by speaking to her, a new language of love pure and full of hope. For many characters in Dubus's work, love is elevated to the spiritual by a transcendental understanding that God is in all things, in the rituals of the Church, in breakfast served by a father, in the welcoming heart of a listening girl.

Dubus returned to his roots in southern Louisiana with the short story "Sorrowful Mysteries" from *The Times Are Never So Bad* (1983), the same collection that includes the final Paul Clement stories. With Paul grown up and married, Dubus turns to young Gerry Fontenot, whose point of view provides an interesting perspective on social injustices that plagued the Deep South in the 1940s and 1950s. Unlike the young Paul, who is uncomfortable with his father, whose self-consciousness cripples his ability to make friends with the popular crowd of boys and whose failure at athletics brings him great shame, Gerry spends long hours with his mother and father, who, unlike the Clements, have a strong marriage. In stark contrast to Paul, Gerry enjoys riding in the car with his parents, fishing and hunting with his father, and going on errands with his mother. With a satisfying home, loved by his parents and cherished by his three older sisters, Gerry is free to worry less about himself and more about the world outside his home. He is aware of World War II, but it affects his life only in the smallest of ways. He notices the ration stamp on his father's windshield. Riding through the countryside with his father, he observes the German prisoners of war sent to work the sugar cane fields. The opening description of the details of war is set against Gerry's sensitive observations of the treatment of "Negros" in his hometown, the poor housing, stemming from low wages, that he notices when he goes with his mother to drop off their washing. The car divides him from the dirt of the badly maintained roads, and he is aware of the "dusty children stopping their play to watch him and his mother in the car, and the old slippers and dress the Negro woman wears, and he . . . looks at her black and brown hand crossing him to take the dollar from his mother's fingers" (124), payment for her laundering their good clothes. He is highly aware of the way Leonard, who comes to mow their summer lawn, is treated; because he is black, he takes his lunch under a tree in the yard, using the same glass and plate that lie separate from the rest of the family's: "they are Leonard's, and from Friday to Friday, they sit, and from fall to spring, and finally forever when one year Gerry is strong enough to push the lawn mower for his allowance," and Leonard comes only when summoned, to collect his Christmas gifts. Gerry never remarks on the fact that his growing stronger takes away the old man's wages. The money Gerry earns buys his way into movies, where there he is aware of the separate door for "Colored," and he wonders if those relegated to the balcony are able to buy the popcorn he enjoys as he watches the Saturday shows. He turns his attention to the matinee heroes, "the strongest and best-looking, the most courageous and good, the fastest with horse and fists and gun" (125), whose adventures he follows in the black and white movies he loves. The reference to the black and white film is a subtle reminder of the issues of race that, just like the balcony, divide his town into black and white. When he leaves the theater, his eyes watch the boys above, and though he smiles in an attempt to make a connection, only one boy ever smiles back.

As Gerry grows older and saves his money for a bicycle and for baseball gloves for the summer afternoon pickup games, he becomes even more aware of the poverty of the town's black citizens, even while his family struggles on his father's salary as a history teacher at the local high school. He worries over his parents' concerns about money, which he overhears when they talk after he is in bed. Nevertheless, he knows that he is privileged well beyond the poor blacks in his town and "feels shamefully rich" when he rides down their streets delivering papers and "wants the boys and girls . . . to know that he only has a new Schwinn because he saved his money to buy it" (128). He lacks the maturity to know how fortunate he is to be able to save and to spend his money on himself, though his perceptive and kind heart knows the injustice of the great racial divide.

The long buildup to the central narrative is a technique that Dubus perfects and uses effectively to provide background information covering long stretches of time that set up and make believable a protagonist's response to a critical moment. For Gerry, that moment comes when he is bested by a black boy who has ridden his bicycle into the white neighborhood, where he watches Gerry and his friends play baseball as they do "every rainless morning except Sunday, when all but the two Protestants go to Mass" (128). Ironically, the same white Christians who never miss the call to worship set and defend the laws that keep down an entire race of people, and Gerry takes it all in. Yet on the ball field that summer morning, they play as equals, their "You're with us" another understated irony in a story full of subtleties, the best one perhaps being the visitor's name: Clay, the substance in the Genesis story that, as all the boys know, was used to make the first man from whom they all descended. The irony again is never explained, never considered by this boy too young to make such a connection. Yet he feels it in his just heart. At the end of the game, outshone by Clay on first base, the position Gerry typically played, he gives away his new Trapper glove, pushing down the "peace and pride in his heart" as he has been taught, though he cannot help it. He will grow into the "Good man" Clay calls him (130).

When a black man Sonny Broussard is sentenced to die for raping a white woman, Gerry turns to his rosary, praying in his bed, feeling for the man so despised. He puts himself in the man's place, holding back a scream at the images that come to him in the dark. Deeply affected by Emmitt Till's lynching, he recounts the facts of the boy's murder, sees his broken body, suffering with his father who, like Gerry, is appalled at such evil. Years later, after driving through long country roads with the girl he plans to marry, he fights a boy in a roadside bar who makes racist remarks. The car has been Gerry's place of learning, where he witnessed the German soldiers and the poor neighborhoods of the black citizens, and now this same car will one day take him out of the South, away from the prejudice he has witnessed all his life. Dubus was deeply affected by the racism of the South, and Gerry and his girlfriend, Camille, are thinly disguised versions of a young Andre and his first wife, Pat. As Gerry drives with Camille back into the "entrance of his town," he watches the road "through the insect-spattered windshield" as he "gazes with burning eyes" (136), his eyes tired from the injustices tolerated by a culture he loves but into which he ultimately cannot fit, each dead insect obscuring his vision home, the place he must finally leave to see his way more clearly in the world.

Dubus's 1986 collection of stories, *The Last Worthless Evening,* includes the second story with Gerry as the protagonist, and as Dubus did, he has joined the military in part to "[flee] the South" and the prejudice there, only to find it again on the USS *Ranger,* the same aircraft carrier from Dubus's first novel, *The Lieutenant,* which will be discussed later in this chapter for its connecting theme of social justice. Gerry has as his bunkmate one of the three black navy men on board. Initially, Gerry struggles with a sense of white guilt, bringing on board and into this small cabin the memories of Emmett Till and his parents' yardman, Leonard, and other stories that shame him as he falls into his Catholic habit of confessing as a way to atone, though the sin is not his. It belongs instead to his race, his white privilege, but Gerry knows that no one can "close [his] eyes to evil without paying a price" (21). Though he had taken a stand in that bar long ago, he is certain that his race will suffer for its acceptance of such prejudice. As he stands his ground while a dropped VT is defused, the metaphorical implication is not lost on him: "The VT fuse at the head of the round is a variable time fuse, meaning once the round is fired from the gun the fuse is activated and will explode not on contact but when it approaches something" (16). He fears the explosion that may come, but he will not abandon his men as he would not back down from racist comments, having gone so far as to pull a knife and put it to a racist's throat. The incident with the VT fuse foreshadows the explosive anger that is sure to come from his bunkmate and friend, who, though he works hard every day to "command" the "demons in his soul" (28), suffers insults and slights without comment until he can take no more. For all of Gerry's social consciousness and in spite of the fact that his father taught history, his own understanding of slavery is naïve, as he attempts to convince Willie that slaveholders did not abuse their property, that economics would not have allowed it. In spite of this, however, Gerry is typical of the protagonists in Dubus's fiction, people who are willing to take a stand against prejudice of any sort, helping to defuse what they can while waiting for the explosion that is sure to come.

When it finally does, with an incident at a party among Gerry, Willie, and a higher ranking officer from Arkansas who expects Gerry to understand his racist point of view because he, too, is white, Willie has to stand by quietly and suffer, knowing that one day he will have to warn his son that his skin color makes him deficient in the eyes of powerful white men who will never see him as "Jimmy" but always as "a nigger" (38). When in frustration and anger Willie erupts and tells his friend of his hatred for white people, "All of you," Gerry, rather than pull away, holds Willie even more tightly, helping defuse the anger at the same time that he determinedly stands apart from the "slave traders and owners and the Klan and murderers and Negro-beaters and those who inflict their torment economically, or with the tongue, or with silence, and eyes that look at a Negro as if he were not even a tree or rain but only air." Physical connection links the two men in a moment of hopefulness, and suddenly, as Gerry writes in his letter to his stateside wife, "he saw not a white man but me" (37). This is the call for social leveling that resonates in many of Dubus's stories, a call for equality among the races and among the sexes so that the country can move peacefully and without fear into a day where no dropped VTs wait to be defused by those who have to risk their lives for social justice. Knowing that equality would be a long time coming, Dubus in his fiction takes his own stand: "Every time we fall into shit, your friend Mr. Fontenot, he's right there with us" (53). In the final moments of the story, as Willie sleeps and Gerry writes, he knows the alarm will soon sound again, and he waits, ready, as Dubus was ready, to take on the difficult social issues of his times. Dubus used his military experiences to confront the injustices he saw in the South and in the larger world just as Gerry forgets the "self" that we turn to at nightfall, opening his eyes to the day's bright promises and sober horrors alike.

Paul Clement joins the marines to prove himself to his father as much as to himself, mirroring the author, as Dubus admitted to many interviewers. His first novel, *The Lieutenant,* is loosely based on his own military experience in the Marine Corps, when he was assigned to an aircraft carrier in the western Pacific. Though "Cadence" serves as a bildungsroman for Paul Clement and while being a marine was transformative for Dubus, the military stories are less significant for the coming-of-age theme that serves as a backdrop than for the common moral concerns that lie at the center of all of his work. The protagonist of *The Lieutenant,* Dan Tierney, has been a marine for four years when the novel opens, and even in his sixth month of service on the USS *Vanguard,* he feels separate from the navy men whom his marines assist on board. He feels, instead, connected to his small unit of men, young and inexperienced as they are, for the very "spirit" (4) that connects them. This sense of detachment from the ship at large provides him with a perspective on military practices that those perhaps too closely connected to them would not notice, and instead of focusing on Dan's growing connection to the larger unit, the novel advances its plot by further isolating Dan as he recognizes and condemns the homophobic practices of military law. The work is worthy of the critical praise it received for its bravery in taking on what was for the time such a controversial subject.

The novel might be criticized for its superficial treatment of women, who all lack the discipline that define his marine detachment. Dan suffers throughout and blames, justifiably, his men's shortcomings on himself as he is distracted by the lack of attention from "his girl" (5) back home who has distractions of her own. He is fascinated by Tolleson's photograph of his stateside girlfriend, seeing in her a "fidelity and promise" (10) that is missing in the face of the young woman whose picture he keeps. He wants from Khristy the same promise, the same pledge of faith that he witnesses in Tolleson's girlfriend. The narrative centers around another of the men whom Dan is charged with commanding, Private Freeman, whose news from home that his fiancé is pregnant stirs in Dan a desire to help and a vision of himself as the boy's savior, as a hero who gives Freeman emergency leave to go home to the girl he loves, a girl whose tentative ties make the boy worry that she will leave him.

Dubus would take up this same narrative thread in "Over the Hill" from his first collection of stories, *Separate Flights.* Private Gale Castete's anxiety over his wife's unfaithfulness leads him to flee his ship, going AWOL to escape for days with a Japanese "butterfly lady" until he is arrested. When he is questioned about why he does not turn to his commanding officer for help, he admits that he does not know, and this despair of not knowing himself or in any way comprehending his life leads him to attempt suicide. Only when facing death does he make the choice to live with the consequences. His sentence in a military prison will cause him to miss the boat out of Japan, and he faces a year away from his wife, who he knows will never wait faithfully. Imagining his life stateside, he accepts the limitations he knows await him and chooses this over death in recognition that it will "be little more than a series of efforts to avoid being deceived. . . . All this stretched before him . . . yet he not only accepted it, but chose it. He figured that it was at least better than nothing" (87). He is left trusting no one, but at least he is able to choose. In her positive review of *Separate Flights,* Joyce Carol Oates focused on Gale's acceptance to help support her conclusion that Dubus's fiction is naturalistic (105). While the stories in *Separate Flights* rarely end happily, arguably a tidy resolution is not their aim. Instead, for the most part, characters do choose, even if sometimes that choice is simple resignation.

The Lieutenant, told from Dan's point of view, is filled with female characters whose lack of development parallels their two-dimensional photographs. On the other hand, the young and inexperienced marines in his unit, many of whom are still in puberty, are all viewed as men, even the "lad" Tolleson, who takes his punishment for insubordination with the frightened eyes of a child. Being a marine means "discipline, it means devotion to duty, it means you do as you're Goddamn told" (9), yet Dan evolves into a better version of himself and becomes the more capable man when he stands against marine and naval law. He favors instead a higher calling to the moral principles that must, for him, trump the military code of conduct. This understanding is typical of many of Dubus's protagonists, who break both secular and spiritual laws for the sake of family or friends.[3] Dan Tinerly will not allow his disillusionment with the military to overcome his sense of responsibility. When he, like Tolleson, speaks insubordinately to his commanding officer, who shows no sympathy for Freeman's plight, Dan is punished and knows that the promotion he has worked hard for will be long in coming. He will not resign from the marines in spite of its flaws. Instead, "he owed it to Freeman to endure as a professional. . . . He had something to give to [future marines]: he could infuse his spirit into training which would make them better men and possibly save their lives as well. That was his final choice . . . he would lead" (196–97). Choosing his men over his own desire to advance in rank leads to a sense of self-respect and responsibility more admirable than what he would have achieved had he blindly followed the rules.

This same willingness to break the law to protect a fellow marine is also the subject of "The Dark Men" in the collection *Finding a Girl in America* (1980). When the investigators from the Office of Naval Intelligence—the name of their unit is used ironically here as their actions suggest nothing but ignorance—appear to investigate Joe Saldi on charges of indecency because of his suspected homosexuality, his friend Captain Devereaux is sent to give him the news. On a day pass, in anticipation of the news to come, Commander Saldi waits in Iwakuni, Japan. As Captain Devereaux's transport moves closer to shore, he watches the carrier, "diminished now but still huge against the sky and the sea beyond." The ship commands the landscape just as its law commands the captain's actions: to give his friend the news that following his nature, loving as he was born to love, has led to his downfall. To bear the passing time before reaching shore, Devereaux closes his eyes, replacing the view of his ship with a more soothing image of "Joe in his flight suit . . . turning his face into the wind. . . . Joe would move on to his plane near the catapult and beyond him the Pacific glittered under the sun, and the endless blue sky waited to lift him up" until he stops, knowing that "memory and imagination would only make it worse," the day's duty almost more than Devereaux's heart can bear (24). He recognizes as truth what he has suspected for the thirteen years that the two have been friends, and when they come together in the officer's club, where they talk and drink, the characters' identifiers switch from names to ranks, for the conversation that follows and the news not spoken but implied are a result of those ranks and the military they serve. Rather than follow through with what he knows his service obligations require, he longs to see Joe free, escaping into a "bright afternoon of tomorrow" (27), where the laws that will sentence him to the shame of a dishonorable discharge cannot reach him.

As in many of Dubus's works, sacred conversation accompanies food and drink, and the two friends have their last meal together as testament to the sacrament of friendship. Once the meal begins, the narrative switches from the identities of rank back to their names, Joe's used again and again as Deveraux struggles to tell his friend of what is to come, looking for a way in between the stories the two tell over their sukiyaki. Joe recounts the tale of a fellow pilot who, fearing that he would not be able to land his plane without crashing, chose to risk it rather than bailing out and going into the water with sharks. His men, who have faith in their pilot, stick with him, and he lands the plane without incident. The story takes on metaphorical weight as Joe becomes the pilot who will not go back to the ship to face the sharks, the dark men whose relentless duty is as cold as their homophobic code of conduct. Instead, when the stories are told and the meal and drinks finished, Joe silently rejects the offer to stand up to the officers and refuse their orders. Instead, he takes to the skies in the plane he has commanded, taking control of his fate and relieving Devereaux of insubordination, going down into the "open sea" where "a swath of gold lay on the water." Closing his eyes, Devereaux imagines "the diving silver plane in the sunset . . . and he saw the low red sun out the cockpit and, waiting, the hard and yielding sea" (30). The lovely colors of the landscape ironically suggest the gold and silver of military badges of honor. Likewise, the plane becomes a metaphor for Joe's life as the automobile has been in many of Dubus's stories where characters take to the open road—here the sky—to make their own fate rather than surrender their will or convictions.

The military can also provide a sense of escape as it did for Paul Clement, who, with his bride, is able to leave behind his parents' marriage and his fear of his father's disapproval; Gerry Fontenot escapes the racism of south Louisiana only to encounter it again in the navy. For Roy Hodges of "The Misogamist," collected as well in *Finding a Girl in America,* the military is a way to escape ties to his fiancé, who waits eight years in Marshall, Texas, forsaking all others in her devotion to him, a devotion that suffocates Roy when he thinks of living out his life as a civilian. In his uniform, he is free to see life as it was meant to be, for he "could not imagine himself performing the concrete rituals of marriage. He did not know what work he would do as a civilian; he did not even want to know." He tells Sheila in letters that he loves her, that he misses her, but he "does not know the extent of [the words'] truth" (52). Only in his uniform does his work have meaning, and this revelation makes him understand "the great division between them" (53). When he does not return for their wedding, the world now at war as Roy is with himself, Sheila is free to begin another life away from Marshall and the empty promises that bound her by a slim hope to a man who could never know or appreciate a woman. Roy saves himself from the pain he causes her by "making her generic, placing her with all the good women who had no real part of his life, so that it wasn't Sheila he was rejecting but cohabitation, and in this brief and cathartic vision he was able to feel as guiltless and purposeful as a monk choosing prayers and a cell . . . though he felt despair at his limitations" (61). Roy's true limitations are never revealed to him as he reduces women to desire, believing that the restrictions on their sexual explorations with an insistence on purity force them into marriage, where they are free to surrender their bodies. Roy cannot see a woman for her whole self. Instead, he reduces women to hunted birds, ground birds, the pheasant and the dove, the bad and the pure, and he writes to Sheila his first real truth, "that he loved his career and he had no place for a wife" (63).

Ironically, it is a woman's point of view from the story "Andromache" (included in *Adultery and Other Choices*), that Dubus uses to illustrate how the military life enlists more than those with commissions. Ellen Forrest is as devoted to the military as her husband, and her days center around the responsibilities that come with being a commander's wife.[4] From the seemingly small but exhausting duties of hosting a Christmas Day party for all the enlisted men under her husband's command to taking on sole responsibility for her household obligations when Joe is in Korea, then later gone again for thirteen months with an infantry battalion stationed in Okinawa, Ellen's daily routine and her every waking thought are determined by the responsibilities that come with being the wife of a major.

The narrative begins with Ellen's having to cope with the news of her husband's death, which came unexpectedly when his transport plane went down. As she lies in bed next to her daughter, unable to sleep because of shock and grief, she holds Posey's hand and imagines her child having to suffer the same fate, of learning to live in the world without her future spouse when he, too, becomes a casualty of war. The story follows a familiar structure that Dubus perfected, opening with a protagonist's first response to tragedy and then backtracking days, sometimes months or years prior to the event, to illustrate how he or she has come to this place in time. As Steve Yarbrough and others have rightly noted, Dubus's stories typically follow one of two patterns: a "straightforward" narration that follows a linear structure or one in which "the thread of the narrative may spin itself first one way, then another" with the focus "not on what is going to happen to the characters; it is instead on what *has* happened to them, on what has made them the people they are" (19). "Andromache" begins with the fact of Joe's death and moves quickly through the four months following as Ellen attempts to adjust to civilian life. Enrolling her two children in schools and learning secretarial skills so that she will be marketable—all of these tasks Ellen does well. Yet her inability to make conversation with civilians who do not relate to her life as a commander's wife makes her seek out a position with Navy Relief, where she will return to Camp Pendleton and the familiarity of its world. Her fidelity to her husband has made her unfit for civilian life, and with this recognition the narrative immediately retreats in time just as Ellen retreats to home movies in order to see her husband alive again. The scene is rich with metaphors. She watches Joe teach their son to ride a bicycle, suggestive of his having taught his boy the navigational skills necessary to pass safely through childhood. Ellen watches him let go as he "called softly: *keep steering, Son, keep steering*" (107). Significant as well is the Old Fashioned cocktail she mixes for herself, drinking it alone in her living room. She has opted for a traditional life and, no matter how hard she tries, she will remain framed by the past, unable to move past her identification as a major's wife.

When the story flashes back in time to her life with Joe, her fidelity to her marriage and to her absolute immersion in her husband's career make her sensitive to the concerns she has for the wives of pilots, those women who lose on average one spouse a year and who are left to mourn without even a body to bury. Despite, or perhaps because of, her intense devotion to Joe, she believes that soldiers *"should be bachelors"* as on the Christmas afternoon she watches through her window a transport plane returning with enlisted men who have had to spend their holiday away from their families (119). These images foreshadow the tragedy to come. Watching the "dark grey seaplane . . . descending toward the water," her "first reaction [is] anger," anger at the families who have had to suspend their celebrations until the men arrive home, of children who have to delay Santa's gifts and the wives who have to serve late dinners, for even Christmas runs on military time (119). At the party for her husband's troops, she and Joe wait for his men, though only a handful attend and most arrive late; most make no appearance at all. Nevertheless, her loyalty to Joe keeps her anger below the surface; she contains her fury at this slight she feels on the part of her husband. As the story title suggests, her devotion to Joe will extend beyond his death, and though she briefly attempts a civilian life, she will return to her familiar world, never really moving beyond that final scene of the story when she receives the bad news. Just as she will later replay the home movies, she loops back into her role as the widowed wife of a major, a fate she accepts for herself and anticipates for her daughter, who, in the final scene she holds "tightly, as if for all time" (126). Posey has inherited her mother's intuition, suggested by her knowing instinctively that her father is dead, her heritage and girlhood having prepared her for the inevitable tragedy that awaits her as she follows her mother's course of loving a military man.

"Corporal of the Artillery," also collected in *Adultery and Other Choices,* shifts the point of view back to a male protagonist who has reenlisted in the Marine Corps, not because he necessarily enjoys the life or finds fulfillment as Roy Hodges does, but because he wishes to escape the debt that comes from having three children in four years of marriage. Ironically, Fitzgerald feels entrapped by the very signing bonus he hoped would free him from constant financial worry. He believes in the recruiter's "fervid sermons," but he ends up feeling betrayed by the promise of "redemption" (85). He spares his wife his uneasiness for he knows she worries enough as she attempts to manage a household on poor pay, though she spends foolishly sometimes to make herself appear a better mother, a more desirable wife. Corporal Fitzgerald, identified first by his rank as all of Dubus's military protagonists are, is weary of the grueling hours that are never his own design. He is economically and biologically trapped, his desire having led to debts that he can only just manage.

Fitzgerald is identified throughout the story by his last name, a fitting reference as this is the name that ties his wife and three children to him, binding him just as his commission has bound him to twenty years of service. His job as scout—observer for a forward observation team—is metaphorically significant as it suggests a man who has perspective, who can see clearly. In fact, he performs his tasks in the field without mistake, but when Carol arrives with their children to collect him after his two-week desert field exercise, he gets into the car without being able to focus. Like the responsibilities that have come on him so rapidly in his twenty-two years, "all of it [happening] so fast and awkwardly that he didn't really see her," he is overwhelmed by his family's expectations, though he works hard to perform each task at home with the same precision he shows in the field (89). Even in bed with his wife, his body seems beyond his control, their lovemaking "over in a rush, before he had even gotten started," just as his youth is prematurely over and just as his satisfaction over paying their bills after his reenlistment was short lived. He wakes with his "palms pressing against the mattress as though to push him upright" (93), the bed becoming a metaphor for the passion that has bound him to her since their first lovemaking in the car.

Just as automobiles are often used to suggest a character's need for escape, those in control of their vehicles in Dubus's stories typically have agency. Fitzgerald's car, however, does not move; it is a make-shift home, a place where his passion is first spent at a drive-in movie in their hometown. In the car with Carol and their children, he does not drive. His wife has control of the wheel as she has control of his life and of what is expected of him. They repeat the patterns of passion, taking the children to a drive-in but not able to stay to the end as their desire for one another causes them to miss the show just as he sometimes feels he has missed other opportunities. After returning home to make love, quickly, Fitzgerald wakes in the darkness, and finally, even if only temporarily, he recognizes that his devotion to his wife is greater than worry, more lasting than debt, more binding even than his commission. Reaching for Carol a second time, their lovemaking "took longer and he was able to marvel and anticipate and remember all at once" (93). In this one moment of existential awareness, Fitzgerald is in control of his time—the past, present, and future—rather than time controlling him, and he is momentarily "grateful and silent, his body sinking into the mattress" rather than attempting to pull away from the quicksand of passion (94). Nevertheless, as with many of the marriage stories, this one concludes with Fitzgerald drawn again into himself. Waking into a new day, he is set apart from his wife, and rather than rise to greet her happiness, he pretends to be asleep. He is not ready yet, and one is left to wonder if he ever will be, if any of Dubus's men who are bound by economic worry and the demands of family can ever be.

Just as the military stories take on the complicated relationships between men and women as well as the intense responsibilities that ranking officers have for the men under their command, three works in three separate collections are equally significant for highlighting the devastating effects of combat on the men called to service during wartime. "The Captain" (collected in *The Times Are Never So Bad*) is a nod to Ernest Hemingway, whose stylistic influence over his work early critics recognized and Dubus readily admitted. In her review of *Separate Flights*, Joyce Carol Oates summed up Dubus's style as "never self-consciously lyric or poetic." Instead "one sees in the craftsmanship of the tales a rigorous paring-back, a concern for what is implied rather than stated, so that the stories as a whole . . . come to operate symbolically, to mean much more than they record" (105). James E. Devlin stated that Dubus "often writes in a prose style made familiar by Hemingway—a style that might be called nonexperimental, American plain style and which often, but not always, suggests a by-the-numbers clarity meant to impose order on chaos" (142). The comparison extends beyond his tendency to suggest rather than pointedly tell. Both writers' characters often depend on ritual, on established patterns of behavior to see them through hard times. As Devlin noted, Dubus's characters often "live by a self-imposed code, trying to establish order and meaning in their lives" (143). In "The Captain," Harry LeDuc, *"Captain LeDuc, retired,"* as his son introduces him to his fellow marines (107), has survived the Korean war, has lived through the horrors of the "Frozen Chosin" and now wears the "colored rectangles of two wars and a wound and one act that had earned him a Silver Star" (108). He knows what his son, Phil, faces. The young man is aptly named as it suggests the love that his father feels for him as well as the camaraderie the young Marine shares with his fellow recruits. Father and son spend a night together, hunting and camping in the woods the day before Phil ships out for his first tour of duty in Vietnam. Before they leave, the two drink together, and his father watches him: "Phil had forgotten who he was and where he was going; was that how the mind survived" (108). Just as Nick Adams in "Big Two-Hearted River" survives by paying attention to the rituals of setting up camp, of pitching his tent, of properly making coffee and breakfast, so, too, does Harry follow set patterns of behavior in cooking the bacon and eggs that become more than just a last meal together, but a sacrament, as the preparing and serving of food to loved ones typically is in Dubus's fiction. Best not to think too much, Dubus's and Hemingway's soldiers conclude. Best, too, not to believe in the possibilities of controlling one's fate through careful living, for his "belief in mystery and chance was too strong . . . . [and] his own mind held images this room of cheerful peace could not contain" (108). So he offers only a little advice to his son. More significantly, he cooks him a meal, efficiently demonstrating the proper techniques. Silently, father and son eat their unseparated eggs from the same pan, a ritual of metaphorical connection, before rising to finish the day. Though he cannot protect his boy from what is to come, he can offer him food just as he provides him with sustaining love. The images of war that could easily consume the father are held at bay for another day, and he walks "out of the trees, into the sunlight" (121), a positive symbol of hope that by concentrating on each task, aware of each moment, he can hold back the horrors of his past and the fears for his son's future.

Duffy, of "Dressed Like Summer Leaves," from *The Last Worthless Evening*, has, simply put, lost his mind. The trauma of the Vietnam War has destroyed his ability to distinguish the real from the imaginary. Suffering from posttraumatic stress disorder, Duffy drinks his days away, further eroding his ability to function normally. The regulars in the dark bar he frequents have long since lost their patience with him, their good will as used up as his credit. With no one to talk to, he stumbles onto the street, where he comes upon Mickey Dolan, an eleven-year-old who, dressed in combat clothes, is confused by the man's behavior and his references to the war and the soldiers whom Mickey's clothes honor. Though Mickey feels forced to spend time in the bar with Duffy, the boy's naïve perspective cannot comprehend how ill the man truly is, even after Duffy mistakes him for the enemy, pushing him and ripping his shirt before another man intervenes. Fortunately, there is a bit of hope that the cycle of violent war may end with the new generation. Rather than remain sick and terrified by what he has witnessed, Mickey leaves the bar having heroically survived battle. The enemy is not the man but the machine of war that broke Duffy's mind, and walking home with his tattered shirt, Mickey knows he will not wear the uniform again.

Like Duffy, Philip Korsmeyer from "The Shooting," one of four military stories in part 2 of *Adultery and Other Choices,* is a mentally ill man whose service responsibilities as well as his duties to his wife and child have unhinged his already fragile mind, and when he finally breaks, he becomes a peacetime military causality. Chuck, a bored sharpshooter who resents that he has never had the opportunity to put his talent to real use, chooses to shoot the young father and husband, this mentally unstable sailor, instead of letting him surrender and get the help he has needed for so long. The navy buries both the reputation of the man and their culpability in the crime under an avalanche of forms that presents a "rock-like segment of truth" with "the appearance or at least the heft of finality" (98). Further insult to Phil Korsmeyer comes from the heroic write-up in the local paper that justifies his death and heralds the man who shot him. The metaphorical truth, however, is found in the descriptions of the newspapers that recount Chuck's moment of glory, "faded yellow as sickness, dry and delicate in his fingers," although he returns to them again and again, handling "them like butterfly wings, fearing for their lives" (105). Jonathan Penner concluded that "The Shooting" is the best in the collection, being a stellar example of what Dubus "cares about: not a man's actions, however dramatic, but their complex effect upon him forever after" (E7). While Chuck is doomed to a lifetime of regret, the media is implicated as well for avoiding the unglamorous truths of war in favor of a story guaranteed to sell papers.

Though Dubus managed to leave the South and resign from the marines, his boyhood in Louisiana and the formative years he spent in the corps were major influences on his fiction. While he would admit that his character Paul Clement was inspired by his own experiences, all his works are in fact shaped in some way by his southern Catholic heritage. In Devlin's artful summary, "Dubus writes of an America of vanishing expectations, a country slipping from postwar confidence, with eroded small cities where jobs are hard to find and pay minimum wage and where the middle class has lost direction as marriages and the church begin to fail" (149). These concerns, of course, permeated all regions of America. While the moral girders of Dubus's fiction have their foundation in his Louisiana Catholic heritage, Dubus's themes are ultimately universally transcendent.

CHAPTER 3

Women and Domestic Space

In a collection of tributes published after Andre Dubus's death, Frederick Busch commented on the respect with which Dubus treated both his craft and those who sought his company hoping to learn something about writing. Busch concluded his essay with the common observation that Dubus "wrote about the soul in its agonies and occasional triumphs. . . . He tried to make beauty. And he succeeded" (Anderson 41). The beauty comes in a variety of ways—from the artfully constructed sentences to the characters' realizations—all of which resonate long after the stories are over. Admittedly, some of Dubus's characters are held back by their place in the world, unable to see beyond their limitations. They are confined by their inability to see their own capabilities and strengths. Still others spiral downward into despair, victims in a seemingly indifferent and hostile world. Many of Dubus's characters are women who find themselves at moments of crisis. Some are able to break through to positive change; others remain trapped within their environments, unchanged and unable to see any possible hope; still others conclude that they alone are to blame for their circumstances and punish themselves without forgiveness. Within Dubus's stories, women from all levels of life struggle to exist within the confines of their domestic environments with varying degrees of success.

Just as the realism that dominates Dubus's narrative technique has been a tendency in American fiction since the mid-1800s, likewise his concern with people's place in society and their struggles to fit into their changing environmental circumstances has been a consistent theme within the American canon. One motif present even in the earliest of American writing has been the use of domestic space and how characters shape or are shaped by their homes and the political and social expectations that make up the mores and habits of home life. Certainly, the metaphors used in creating the motif of domestic space have been various and many; these also have changed over time. Nevertheless, the home and its importance as both backdrop for and extension of the self have been evident from the earliest of sketches. Dubus's stories are often framed by domestic concerns while his characters' autonomy or lack thereof is suggested by their relationship to their domestic space. Thomas Kennedy has stated that "each of Dubus's women face . . . a challenge to self-knowledge as a stage in the bridging of human isolation, or in succumbing to it, in being lost to hunger, or progressing beyond hunger to love as a higher state of existence" (*Andre Dubus* 23). Many such stories can be termed naturalistic in that the women protagonists are bound by their environment or restricted by their biological or sociological limitations to the point that they do not recognize that they have sovereignty in matters that affect their own lives. These women are best defined by their containment, spaces of fear or control, depression or despair. Each victimized by a trauma in her life, these women either struggle in vain or surrender to their hopelessness, unable to see any possible chance for change. In "Leslie in California," "Rose," and "Anna," women struggle within the confines of negativity in homes that are the antithesis of the domestic ideal. In postmodern American fiction, the home is in crisis, and the resulting chaos is the theme of these three stories. In "Waiting" and "Killings," women protagonists have either been traumatized by domestic experiences beyond their control or they wait passively for transcendence from their pain, a deliverance they do not seem actively able to pursue. In "The Pretty Girl," though Polly attempts to create a new life for herself that expands the boundaries of her past limitations, she is trapped by the passivity that her beauty affords her. How all of these women survive within such negative limits becomes the central issue of these stories, which span Dubus's canon.

Juanita Jody Joury Creehan in "Waiting," from the 1980 collection *Finding a Girl in America,* wants to give in to the power of transcendence, yet her true desire is to surrender to the pull of suicide. Having for twelve years suffered the grief of her young husband's death, Juanita cannot seem to create any meaning in her life. Instead, she lives alone in a small apartment, sleeping as late as she can so that she has only a little of the day to make it through before evening, when she goes to work as a waitress in a local bar. She lives near Camp Pendleton, near the marine base where her husband was stationed. When he was killed in Korea, she was left with few friends and no will to make more. Instead, Juanita's life has collapsed into a series of meaningless days and nights that run together. Her solitude and isolation lead her to contemplate killing herself.

In the years following her husband's death, Juanita has lived alone with the memory of Patrick's death. Though she could not know exactly how he died, she had pieced together what facts she had and embroidered them with details that fill her mind as she drifts off to sleep each night. She gets as much information as she can from her husband's marine friend Starkey, and what he cannot tell her, she creates for herself: "Some nights she descended further into the images" (91). Sleep and the memories of her husband, whether real or imagined, become the escape she needs from the stifling confines of her life. Alone in her apartment with her grief, she feels incapable of anything more than the artificial smiles she puts on when she meets her customers at work.

On the evening of the present action, Juanita reaches out to a man who has watched her most of the night at her job. At work, she goes to the bathroom to study her reflection in the mirror, his intent looks prompting her to take a long study of herself. From there, she agrees to his following her home, and for the first time in her life, "she woke with a man and had to remember his name" (92). For the first time since her husband's death, she has reached out to another man. They had shared drinks at her kitchen table the night before, Juanita opening her house as a way to connect beyond the memories of her husband, as a way to avoid the sleep she usually craves. However, when morning comes, she is uncomfortable with him there and does not want to extend their connection. In fact, she breaks it by getting up and leaving her house in the dark and driving to the ocean.

For Juanita, the beach has become another way to escape or to fill her meaningless days. With no roles, no routine beyond her night job serving people in temporary moments of inconsequential connection, Juanita uses swimming and body surfing and walking on the beach in the cold weather as a way to pass the time. However, on the particular morning when she has awoken beside and escaped from the sergeant major whom she leaves sleeping in her bed, she spends most of her time at the beach thinking of her high school friend who had killed himself years before. As with her husband's death, Juanita had created details surrounding the suicide, seeing him "in a dirty and disorderly room, sitting on the edge of his bed and reaching that moment when he wanted more than anything else not to be Vicente" (93). The apartment she creates for him in her mind reflects how she sees his life, lacking a nurturing caretaker, overrun, just as he had been, by hopelessness. When she had heard of her friend's death, she had wondered if he had thought about the next day and if that might have helped him: "The word tomorrow stayed in her heart. She saw it in her mind, its letters printed across the black and white image of Vicente sitting on the bed with the pistol" (93). To rid herself of the pain of the news, she reaches out to her husband, undressing him, combating death by making love.

However, on the summer day in 1963, as she walks on the beach and remembers Vicente and her husband while struggling to remember the name of the man in her bed, she steps into a "shallow pool left by the tide" (93). Metaphorically, this action suggests Juanita's life as she plays along the edges, wading into the shallows of memory that the death of her husband has left her. As she steps in, she is looking out toward the sea. As she steps out, she has a memory of her first year without her husband, trying to sleep, waiting for the pills that she used every night to take effect, "the first signals in her fingers, her hands: the slow-moving dullness, and she would touch her face, its skin faintly tingling; going numb, then she was aware only of the shallow sound and peaceful act of her slow breathing" (93). The descriptions of falling asleep coming at this point in the narrative work to suggest her desire for permanent sleep as, in the present action that follows, she is riding a wave, its colors the same black and white as her image of Vicente's death. The images suggest her giving over to the effects of the sleeping pill: "Breaking it took her with head down and outstretched arms pointing, eyes open to the dark and white foam" (95). The wave moves her onto the shore, but it also recedes. Thomas Kennedy likewise recognized the importance of Juanita's connection to the sea "as a symbol of the oblivion that will one day be granted her, for which she waits not without a shade of welcome, perhaps not without an intention to hasten that day's arrival" (*Andre Dubus* 15). Left with only the shallow pools of memory, Juanita has given up hope. She had been a passionate girl who had for years defined herself by her relation to the boys and men in her life. Her name, half her very self, comes from her father and husband, and without this frame of reference, she is left with an emptiness to which she has been resigned for twelve years.

The shift in the story comes with the realization that Juanita will most likely kill herself, ending her long time of loneliness and suffering. She has spent years surfing the tide, riding out her emptiness on the beach. The unnamed man with whom she temporarily connects will not be able to bridge her pain. She tells him the story of Vicente, cataloguing her history in the same way that she had read the facts of her friend's obituary, admitting that she waits to die: "Like I sneaked into the movie and I'm waiting for the usher to come" (96). Death will come for her; the question is if she will wait for the show's natural end or be escorted out in the middle.

The final image of the story suggests that Juanita will forego sex without marriage, the only sin she ever believed herself capable of committing, for a new and final one. In fact, the absence of passion has only compounded her grief. Meaningful connection with another human being would help her, maybe save her from suicide. Yet, as she admitted to herself years before, she is not capable of help anymore. In the final scene, she surrenders to sleep, and in what she calls a "near-dream," a more willed action than simply dreaming, she sees herself standing naked in the water, the sexual images suggesting that this is the only fulfillment her body is capable of anymore: "She saw herself standing naked in the dark waves. One struck her breast and she wheeled slow and graceful, salt water black in her eyes and lovely in her mouth, hair touching sand as she turned then rose and floated in swift tenderness out to sea" (96). She sees herself giving into the waves and their caresses, riding them out, surrendering to death as she has surrendered to grief. Unable to redefine the possibilities of "tomorrow" (93), she gives in, overwhelmed.[1]

Ruth Fowler, from "Killings," also collected in *Finding a Girl in America*, is likewise unable to deal with the grief she feels following her son's murder. Home from college for summer vacation, Frank, her youngest son, had taken a job as a lifeguard at the beach where he met Maryann. In the wake of the shooting, Matt Fowler, Ruth's husband, from whose point of view the story is told, recognizes that though he is trying to move forward with his life, his wife has been overwhelmed by her son's death. She is trapped by grief, existing in a vacuum, rarely leaving her home, her pain exacerbated by the court system's having released her son's killer on bail. Buying aspirin and cigarettes to help herself cope, Ruth sees Richard at the drugstore, where she hides in the back, waiting for him to leave. Matt tells his friend Willis that "she sees him too much. . . . It's killing her" (4). Matt knows his wife has become a prisoner in her own home, fearing the boy she would shoot herself "if she thought she could hit him" (5). She confesses her pain to her husband: "At nights in bed she would hold Matt and cry, or sometimes she was silent and Matt would touch her tightening arm, her clenched fist" (10). For a while, she is hopeless in her sorrow, believing that no justice will be served against her son's murderer, that his twenty-year sentence will never be enough. When Matt decides to avenge his son's death, she gives her consent by remaining silent, by willing him to do for her what she cannot do for herself.

Unlike many of the married couples depicted in Dubus's fiction, the Fowlers have a strong union. When tragedy strikes with their son's death, Ruth turns to Matt in bed "where she had during all of their marriage told him of her deepest feelings: of love, of passion, of fears about one of the children, of pain Matt had caused her or she had caused him" (7). When Matt returns from killing his son's murderer, Ruth listens to her husband and tries to comfort him in the most personal way, by making love with him. As Lucy Ferriss has pointed out, "for Dubus' women . . . expressions of love through another human being, whether erotic or maternal, is itself a kind of prayer or communion with the holy" (236). That Ruth feels no remorse for what Matt has done is clear in her opening up to him, desiring to comfort him: "She was holding him, wanting him, and he wished he could make love with her but he could not. . . . Holding Ruth, his cheek touching her breast, he shuddered with a sob that he kept silent in his heart" (20). The two are separated by the gulf of their feelings. Ruth believes that he has done the right thing. However, she will never fully understand her husband's suffering, the guilt he feels over murdering someone's son, someone's lover; therefore, she is cut off from the most sustaining power in her life.

Dubus's story "Leslie in California," from his 1983 collection *The Times Are Never So Bad,* is told from the perspective of a young woman who has moved west, leaving on the far coast her father and friends to begin a new life with her husband, Kevin. Leslie expects her marriage to be full of opportunities; however, once she arrives in California, she begins to wonder if she will be one of those women she has read about who end up "dead in her kitchen" (83). Phyllis Rosser has pointed out that "art in the [nineteen] seventies revealed that for many women home had become a war zone of violence and male abuse. Male violence was creating psychological trauma in its victims that was identical to the 'shellshock' experienced in war, says Harvard psychiatric professor Judith Lewis Herman" (61–62). Leslie has been reduced by a paralyzing fear that renders her unable to make necessary decisions. As Madonne Miner has argued, "Leslie presents herself and her situation quietly, flatly, without emotion as if she and the woman she describes are two different people. That distancing, I would argue, is right: it represents exactly the feelings of a woman who comes face-to-face with the fact that her husband is a batterer—and she, a battered wife" ("Jumping" 24). Though she knows that she should flee, she is able to transcend her space only through memory and wishes.

Donald Junkins has examined Ernest Hemingway's "principles of composition," which followed the ideas outlined in Ezra Pound's *ABC of Reading.* "Hemingway wrote with his ear and his eye," charging "language with meaning to the utmost degree," Junkins stated. Dubus created meaning in this same way. Junkins summarized the three processes: "1. Throwing the object on to the visual imagination; 2. inducing emotional correlation by the sound and rhythm of the speech; and 3. inducing both of these effects by stimulating the associations (intellectual or emotional) that have remained in the receiver's consciousness in relation to the actual words or group of words employed" (18). As Junkins pointed out, Hemingway used words that are not "ideationally thematic, but implicatively thematic" (19). While images may not "denote" anything but setting, they "connote" a particular mood or feeling.[2] Dubus and Hemingway shared this technique. Like Hemingway, Dubus used imagery in the opening paragraphs of his stories to connote a mood that sets up the conflict that follows. Images echo, and key words elevate setting to compound that mood, providing a deeper understanding of each character's dilemma. Setting is used not just for backdrop; rather, it is carefully constructed to arouse empathy, and Dubus's work often uses the motif of domestic space to suggest a character's sense of self. Leslie is primarily dominated and characterized by the overwhelming threats that define her sense of space. She lives in fear of her husband, whose treatment of her grows more violent the longer they are together. Each detail of the opening paragraph works to set up the conflict. The descriptions of Leslie's domestic space illustrate her lack of autonomy. With the first words, an alarm rings to awaken her to a morning "black and grey" (81). The alarm is a portentous warning as the horrors of her life are revealed in the second sentence: "I smell Kevin's breath and my eye hurts and won't open" (81). These details, given in tandem with no dividing mark of punctuation, emphasize that when Kevin drinks, Leslie gets hurt. The third sentence likewise combines a description of his movements with the smell of alcohol: "He gets out of bed, and still I smell beer in the cold air." Kevin is "naked" (81), an atavistic detail compounded by other such descriptions throughout the story that are filtered through Leslie's point of view.

Though Leslie layers herself against the cold and fear, attempting vainly to warm and protect herself by putting on a robe, she must go "by flashlight to the kitchen" (81). Living without power might be enough to worry any new wife, but Leslie has more serious concerns. She is unable to bring herself to action, and her own lack of power is mirrored by her home, a rented place as unfamiliar to her as her present condition. Moving through the first paragraph, Leslie remains disconnected from her surroundings. She is cut off from nature: "Birds are singing, or whatever it is they do," she thinks to herself. Without hope for a better day than the night before has promised, Leslie feels disassociated from the landscape outside her home. Afraid and cut off from others, from any sense of community, she escapes her present dilemma through mental journeys. Her mind moves from the present to memories of her childhood as rapidly as a bird's flight, an imagistic pattern used throughout the story. She remembers "New England mornings with the lights on and a warm kitchen and catching the school bus," a safe scene where leaving is possible (81). Her mind continues to move from the frightening reality of her present existence with Kevin to the safety of her previous life. When she thinks about Kevin's being gone from the house, she moves into thoughts of her father and the happy promises and hopes that he had for her marriage.

Leslie's disconnection is accentuated by the fragmented prose. Present details are set against the comforting memories of her childhood without transition. Sentences are short and the phrasing is choppy, reinforcing Leslie's tension. Like Hemingway, Dubus uses a combination of short, jerky sentences with lyrically soothing ones to suggest Leslie's state of mind. When she is thinking of her father, of her safe and happy childhood, the sentences are longer and more melodious. When she is in present time, aware of her abusive husband and her violent marriage, the fragmented prose mirrors her fragmented spirit. Before the first paragraph is over, the truth of Leslie's life is revealed. Though she came to California with the same positive hopes that her father had for her, the life that she is leading only four months later is full of violence. In the last sentence of the opening paragraph, she hears Kevin coming into the kitchen, and she stands "at the stove so [her] back is to the door" (81). Her body language reveals that she will not leave her marriage, a fact confirmed throughout the story.

She survives the morning by following a routine. She fixes Kevin the breakfast she knows he craves when he has a hangover, using the familiarity of her past waitressing job to get by until he leaves, and, alone, she can look at her bruised face in the bathroom mirror. Her only confrontation with Kevin is the single statement: "I wish you didn't hit me last night . . . and the two before that" (84). She can only wish and dream, vacillating between what she wants to do and what she begins to know she will not. Wanting some order in her world, she thinks of cleaning her house. Then, moving from her living room to "open the front door," she stands there, looking "out through the screen" (84). Just as Leslie can see out, knowing what it takes to get out, she is held back by the screen, just as her ties to Kevin and her fear of him entrap her.

Her only escape comes in memories of her father, when she felt safe as a child in her New England home. Her father was her protector at Camp Pendleton, where, when she was a girl, she had tried to pet a bobcat. Leslie's memories of animals are frightening. She remembers the big horse her sister rode during her "lessons in New England; I watched her compete, and I was afraid, she was so small on that big animal jumping" (82). The narrative placement of these details, coming so soon after Leslie's atavistic descriptions of Kevin, reveals that Leslie's fear has transferred to her own life. She is "so small" and defenseless in her marriage and wants her father to call her back from danger as he did long ago. She imagines rattlesnakes on the lawn with the birds and the surrounding hills filled with armed men tracking bobcats.

Leslie's feelings of hopelessness are intensified by her isolation. "Movement," Doreen Massey has stated, "categorizes postmodern society" and "has made it difficult for people to retain any sense of a local place. . . . An idealized notion of an era when places were supposedly inhabited by coherent . . . communities is set against the current fragmentation and disruption" (146). Though there are houses nearby where Leslie might seek help, she "can't see any of them" (84). Her lack of perspective suggests her unwillingness to journey into the hills where she might get help. Then thinking of "filling a canteen and walking, maybe all morning," she soon remembers the men who hunted for a bobcat the day before, an animal that has reportedly killed "someone's child"

(85). Leslie, too, is someone's child, and while her father was there to protect her from the bobcat at Camp Pendleton all those years ago, he is now living far away on another coast, available to her only in memories. A shadow spreads across the yard, a warning that time is passing. In spite of Kevin's eminent return, Leslie's last thought suggests her inability to leave: "I shut the screen and look around the lawn where nothing moves" (85). Nothing moves just as Leslie cannot presently bring herself to leave, her only escape the comforting memories of her father.

For Andre Dubus's characters defined by their domestic space, home may evoke security and stability against the uncertainties of the modern landscape or, conversely, may serve as a place of entrapment, as it is for Leslie and as it is for the protagonist of "Rose," collected in the 1986 volume *The Last Worthless Evening,* whose story is filtered through a first-person narrator who is, as Kennedy has called him, a "student of the human spirit" (*Andre Dubus* 45). The perspective was a way for Dubus to distance himself from such a person, as he would tell interviewer David Yandall Todd: "I must have written a note, 'Tell it from the point of view of a narrator listening to the woman years later. Put it down in a local bar and let it go.' I couldn't go into the point of view of someone who would allow abuse of a child—or abuse one—until later in the story" (Gresham 183). What the narrator comes to understand is that Rose is asleep to the power of possibility. She is unable to see that her actions redeemed her, freed her. She can only focus on what she did not do; so, believing herself defenseless against the courts, she loses her children without a fight. In an effort to come to terms with Rose and her unwillingness to believe in herself, the narrator creates a past for her. Though Leslie has the strength of her childhood to draw on, positive memories of home into which she can retreat from the horrors of her present life, Rose does not offer her storyteller any clue as to what her earliest experiences were, no hint that her life was ever any different. And just as Leslie has been transformed from "somebody's child" (*Times* 82), someone loved and cherished and protected, to someone who fears for her life, the narrator in "Rose" is not so naïve that he does not understand that she might have had a positive upbringing herself, though she gives no sign. From interactions with customers who attend the local private college, he has come to realize that the privileges of wealth, be they spiritual or material, do not always guarantee safe passage through a world with such power to corrupt and ultimately damage. "Sometimes," he begins, "when I see people like Rose, I imagine them as babies, as young children" (179), as all people might envision the sad characters who enter their lives, searching "the aging skin of the face, the unhappy eyes and mouth" for a clue as to the beginning of their downfall, the answer to the riddle of their misery (179).

This frame sets up what becomes the story of Rose's life and is especially effective in its ability to emphasize the narrator's and Dubus's belief that all human beings are combinations of their past and present environments. In setting up the one defining story, the one experience he knows has shaped Rose and brought her to Timmy's as a regular to drink alone, or at best to make quiet talk with the person who sits next to her, the narrator moves first through the years that he believes shaped her, made her, determined her sense of self. Rose, however, evaluates and defines herself only by moments of shame, never able to shake her self-doubt: "Her face, sober or drunk or on the way to it, looks constantly watched, even spoken to, by her own soul. Or by something it has spawned, something that lives always with her, hovering near her face" (181). In her judgment of herself, she concludes that she is guilty and deserves the very worst as perhaps others have deserved the very best. The narrator spends a great deal of time insisting that the audience empathize with the heartache Rose has suffered and continues to endure.

In a side story that the narrator tells in order to set up the principal narrative, he speaks of a marine recruit who failed basic training in spite of the fact that when he was sleepwalking, he was capable of all the feats of strength that defeated him when he awoke. It is "consciousness," the narrator concludes, that was his enemy (185). His awareness of his thin body made him believe that he could not accomplish what the sergeant put before him, though many small-framed young men made it through. He is bested, beaten because he never believed that he was capable of having the strength to withstand what was expected of him. He left without knowing that he failed because he did not know the truth about himself, that he had the physical capability to succeed and that self-perception alone created his failure.

These same lies make up the whole world, the narrator concludes, and lull people into believing that money or beauty or physical strength can save them by giving them the confidence it takes to withstand whatever those in authority expect. The rest, those without money or beauty or physical strength, are left without even the lies to pull them through whatever expectations or obstacles confront them. This is Rose's story, and she tells it to the narrator one January night at the close of the week, just as she is nearing the end of what she believes to be her failed life. She faces him across the corner of the bar, where she has been propelled by people pushing her out, squeezing "in beside her." She gives in to their pressures without resistance. This simple description becomes a metaphor for the complex series of events that "wedge" her out of her life, that strip her of everything consequential and leave her feeling too weak and undeserving to fight (189). She is never aware of her possibilities and believes that the mother who went to battle for her children's safety was only a fleeting version of herself. Like the marine, she is asleep to her own power. In this failure to believe in herself, to accept being pushed aside, she loses her home and family and, consequently, herself.

Timmy's has become a home for Rose, a safe community against the dangers of the outside world. Having lost her family, she has no friends, no one to confide in, except the narrator, who has become the one person to whom she trusts enough to tell her story, at first speaking "as though we were talking in symbols" (189). Initially, she speaks of her fears, about fires in winter, about "the sirens" that go by all "the time in winter" (190), about how easy it is to slip and break a bone. Sirens and fire, broken bones and fear—all these clues begin to mount up. "They remind me," she tells the narrator. "Sometimes it isn't even the sirens. I try not to think about anything. Or I'm at work. . . . Or I'm going to sleep. Or right now, just then, we were talking about winter. I try not to think about them. But here they come, and I can see them. I feel them. Little flames. Big ones" (190). Here, memory serves very differently than it does for Leslie, who opens the door of her mind to happy thoughts of her father and the security of his kitchen, of mornings getting ready for school and breakfast and the lights on. For Rose, domestic memory is awash with flames, of failure at home even in the face of what the narrator comes to see as an obvious victory. Yet Rose is not capable of sustaining that moment of triumph any more than the sleeping marine can carry his strength into his waking day.

The narrator's empathy is heightened because of his having lost a child in a car wreck. Rose, too, feels that she lost her children through some sort of inner weakness that failed her. She knows that she saved their lives for the moment and that her actions were monumental: "It's the only thing I ever did. In my whole fucking life. The only thing I ever did that was worth a shit" (191). What the narrator comes to understand first through Rose telling her story and then his retelling it is that in her thirty minutes of action, she was redeemed. Kerstin W. Shands has noted a telling point: "The public sphere has been seen as an arena open to state regulation and control, whereas the private sphere is supposedly an area of freedom from state interference, but as Nancy Duncan has argued, 'The private is a sphere where those families who are not dependent on the state for welfare have relative autonomy. Those who are dependent, however, are often subject to unwarranted intrusion and surveillance'" (63). Because Rose is reliant on the state for her defense, her financial weakness adds to her inability to withstand its authority. She is doomed to drink alone, to live alone, to jangle with fear when she hears sirens, drawn back in time to the flames that essentially consumed her. Without the narrator's translating the events, the story would never be fairly told, for Rose "could not see . . . and still cannot" that she "redeemed herself, with action" (214). Dubus told Bonnie

Lyons and Bill Oliver that he "heard Rose speak, telling her story" and that "the real truth for me was that she was redeemed; she just didn't know it. She had been made to feel powerless by forces that were too much for her: hard work, hard living, no future. But finally she did the right thing; she defied her husband, she saved her children" (150). Nevertheless, when the moment is over, she goes back to her powerlessness. She allows the state to take her children, and she never forgives herself.

Before he begins any of the details of the fateful night or Rose's early years with her husband, Jim, the narrator focuses on the clock at Timmy's, pointing out that it is always set twenty minutes ahead. Though the bartender can manipulate the hour by simply moving a clock's hand, Rose's most challenging opponent as she struggled to be a good mother was her inability to master time. The extra hour at the grocery store, the extra attention to her children, the spare moment to answer their questions—she needed time for the patience necessary to deal with their curiosity, their toddling off from the grocery cart to pick up colorful boxes. But Rose did not have any time between the laundry and the schedules that were never on track. Rather, daily "she felt that the other women, even those with babies, with crawling and barely walking children, with two or three children, and one pregnant with a third, had about them some grace, some calm, that kept their voices soft, their gestures tender; she watched them with shame, and a deep dislike of herself" (196). She felt that she was a failure, the only mother who did not measure up to the pressures of the world. Yet the narrator vicariously walks each step of her bone-tired day so that when the night of the sirens comes, he can fully understand.

Rose and Jim began to change soon after they married, and as time passed, the more the demands of family became impossible for Jim to meet. When he came home to his apartment, he saw the clothes drying on the curtain rod and backs of chairs as accusers, pointing out his failure to provide the basics for his family. He tried to create order by removing the clothes and finding a place to rest, until "he stood in some corner of the bedroom, the bathroom, in the last place in his home that was his" (197). Without a place to fortify himself, he drank more until, like Kevin, he began to lash out: "He struck the boy first, before contraception and the freedom and new life it promised" (197). He reacted against his three-year-old son as he blamed his children for the problems in his life. When she heard the first slap, Rose was in the kitchen a metaphorical space used ironically here. Rather than using it as a place of nourishment, Rose uses her kitchen to escape into her domestic tasks. When she saw the accusing look on her son's face for not defending him against his father, in that moment "she felt something fall between herself and her son" that was "infinite, and she could never cross it again" (198). She was distanced from her boy, no longer connected by her role as mother though she continued to fulfill the immediate and necessary needs of her children. Instead of taking action against Jim, Rose forgave him his violence though she "could no longer feel love, or what she had believed love to be" (202). However, when Jim breaks their son's arm, she is yanked from her thoughts of dishes and laundry and finds her voice, one that "grew, its volume [filling] the world" (205) until Jim turned on her instead.

When she takes action, ultimately fleeing a burning apartment and running down her husband with their car, Rose finds the strength that had been dormant within her all those years. Though she saves her children, she loses them in court; in fact, "before the trial, before she even left the hospital, she had lost the children. . . . They all went to the same foster home. She did not know where it was" (212). An observation by Shands yields insight into Rose's dilemma: "The spatial boundaries affecting, defining, or determining women's lives are thus both material and metaphorical, involving both the literal, concrete confinement of women in actual domestic space and conditions that are measurable in society at large, that is, legal and economic forms of discrimination that keep women in certain spaces" (63). Rose surrendered to the state and lost her children, shattered by "the life she chose [which] slowly turned on her, pressed against her from all sides, invisible, motionless but with the force of wind she could not breast" (214). Her passivity overshadows her courage, and she is defeated.

Dubus reemphasized the tremendous impact of one's relationship to home in "Anna" from *The Times Are Never So Bad*. The short story focuses on a young woman who, like Rose, is afraid to act. Anna's negative containment is due in part to her commitment to her boyfriend, who has little ambition. Wayne flips burgers at Wendy's and is not motivated enough even to buy more than the one white shirt required by management, in spite of the hassle his laziness causes Anna, who makes sure every night that the shirt is laundered or at least set to air. Anna takes on all of the domestic responsibilities in an attempt to turn her apartment into a home, a place where she and her partner can build a future. While Wayne is floating through life, entertained by what is in front of him, Anna wants to extend the satisfaction that she feels when she is at work into her domestic world. Judith Fryer has noted that in "America, there is a long-standing tradition that describes the tension between [private space and public space] and that defines the private space as the realm of the imagination, and the public space as the realm of behavior" (9). Anna feels, for the most part, confident and in control at work, and she wants to prolong those feelings of autonomy. She dreams of a private space as nurturing as her public world, a home with set rules of performance that would provide her family with the rituals of positive routines.

As in many of Dubus's stories, the opening paragraph reveals important points about the protagonist. Anna's last name is "Griffin," a mythical beast that is half eagle, half lion; in addition, her hair is changing color, now part brown and part blonde. The description of her face is divided into left and right. Even her first name is a palindrome, divisible into two mirrored parts. These details given together work to suggest that Anna is in a liminal state, emerging into a new self. Though dissatisfied with her looks, however, she will not color her hair as she is waiting to see how it will turn out. She does not see that she is already pretty, that the two parts of her face come together in a way that is pleasing; instead, "the light of her eyes, the lines of her lips seemed bent on denial" (137). Her lack of confidence makes her unable to see her physical power. Though she wants more than Wayne is capable of offering, instead of leaving, Anna seems content to see how things will turn out. Her domestic space reflects that the outcome is not hopeful.

Anna is still young, only twenty, but her life with Wayne is aging her quickly, as evidenced by her reaction to her home when she gets off work every day. Leaving her job at Sunnycorner convenience store, she feels a negative shift from the satisfaction that work provides. Though she is filled with energy after the physical restrictions of standing behind a counter all day, sometimes "she felt something else too, as she stepped outside and crossed that line between fatigue and energy: a touch of dread and defeat" (139). She comes home to an apartment of other people's "leavings," a few pieces of furniture that are mismatched and old (139). Along the way, she passes the same sights every day, and she details the scenery, the cooking smells that inhabit her building, which "bother her because it was a daily smell" (139). Already at twenty Anna is bored by her empty domestic routines. She and Wayne live day to day rather than working toward a future. Madonne Miner has made the point that the story is one "of crossing a line between energy and fatigue, between working-class female adolescence and working-class womanhood. It is a story . . . about the near impossibility of individualized desire on the part of someone like Anna" ("Jumping" 20). It is ultimately a story about class, and her home, in which she feels defeated, is a daily reminder of her station. When Anna awoke in the mornings, she "saw the place clearly with its . . . tossed clothes, beer bottles, potato chip bags. . . . and sometimes later, during the day or night, while she was simply crossing a room, she would suddenly see herself juxtaposed with the old maroon couch which had been left . . . by whoever lived there before she and Wayne. . . . and she felt older than she knew she ought" (139). Anna's apartment is a reflection of her current life, seemingly temporary and thrown together without much evidence or hope for change. Though Anna may want more than robbing drugstores with Wayne will offer, she hesitates to articulate her own plans or to let him know directly how she feels. Instead, like Rose and Leslie, she goes through the motions, playing her role while making the best of what she has before her, passively waiting to see how things will turn out.

However, during the robbery, there is a shift in the action that moves Anna from childhood into a new, more adult role as Wayne's partner. When she waits in the car while Wayne holds up the druggist at knifepoint, she clearly sees herself in the moment. She watches Wayne through the snow and feels "doomed": "Stripped of history and dreams, she knew only her breathing and smoking and heartbeat and the falling snow" (140–41). Her connection to Wayne and their empty life have made her, like Leslie, unable to see past the present moment into a better tomorrow. Miner's critique affirms this assessment: "Without past or future, she is a woman for whom self-imagination proves difficult, for whom self-vision is restricted to the present tense and present physical situation" ("Jumping" 22). With nothing to look back on, no positive experiences from her past to draw on for strength, she is equally hopeless regarding her future. She remains in the moment, focusing on her actions and reactions, judging both herself and Wayne.

When the robbery is over, Anna wants to go to Timmy's, the makeshift home where she feels happy and welcomed by friends: "It was the only place outside of her home where she always felt the comfort of affection" (143). She shares a good feeling of togetherness with the regulars at the bar just as she shares a strong physical connection with Wayne, whom she loves and to whom she is attracted. Nevertheless, she is weakened by her passion as she is not willing to sacrifice her desire for him to make more of her life. This conflict in feeling is mirrored by Anna's actions at the bar as she constantly thinks of doing one thing but resorts to another, from the simple decision of whether to go to the bathroom or smoke another cigarette or finish a shot. Though she would like a job at Timmy's, where she might combine the satisfaction of work with the affection of friends, she doubts that she could learn to be a bartender. She lets her insecurities overwhelm her: "I don't think I could remember all of the drinks" (144). In fact, when she is with Wayne, Anna often does have a hard time focusing, seeming to act without thinking or thinking about something other than her actions. Her manner reflects her inability to confront the issue of their dead-end life.

Nevertheless, though her job at Sunnycorner does not provide her the connectedness she so desires, she does feel a confidence in herself when she is on the job, alert, paying attention to each detail, careful not to make a mistake, and proud of herself when she does not. Unlike the escape she seeks at Timmy's, Anna feels in control, which allows her to dream of a life different from the one she has with Wayne. When the bank tellers come into the store, she imagines the homes they have: "She gave them large, pretty apartments with thick walls so that they only heard themselves; stereos and color televisions, and soft carpets and soft furniture and large brass beds; sometimes she imagined them living with men who made a lot of money, and she saw a swimming pool, a Jacuzzi" (138). Unlike the apartment that Anna shares with Wayne, these women, though they live with men, have comfortable places that reflect their autonomy and give them a confidence that Anna does not feel. By comparison, thoughts of her own residence weaken her so that "when the tellers were at the counter, she was shy" (138). She sees these women empowered by their homes while she feels defeated in comparison.

After the robbery, as Anna stands in front of the stereos and televisions, she is one step closer to having the apartment that she had envisioned for the bank tellers, yet when it comes time to make the purchases, she is not interested. That she is not a thief by nature is clear when she remembers to take money to work to pay for her coffee and donuts and cigarettes. She takes satisfaction in her register balancing at the end of her shift and, knowing the value of a hard day's work, feels bloated by their heavy spending. Her desire to be like those women she admires extends no further than desire. She would rather do without, she learns, than steal: "She was sad. She watched Wayne and remembered him running out of the drugstore and . . . she was ashamed that she was sad and felt sorry for him because he was not. . . . She wanted to cry" (152). In the mall, she feels separate from Wayne, who selects the stereo, the television, the records, while Anna is powerless to voice her unhappiness. As Miner pointed out, "just as she cannot put herself into the deep carpeted apartments she imagines for the bank tellers. . . she cannot put herself into a . . . discussion about guarantees. Instead, she puts herself imaginatively in her own apartment, sees herself cooking and sweeping. Within the confines of this picture, she is finally able to generate a statement of desire" ("Jumping" 22). Her involvement takes shape in the form of a vacuum cleaner, evidence of her longing to put things right, to improve her domestic space as best she can: "She did not know what she was waiting for, but standing on the sidewalk as Wayne's head and shoulder went into the car, she was anxious and mute" (153). As he reaches in to remove their purchases, bought with the stolen money, Anna never articulates her feelings; instead, she retreats silently into the apartment, feeling the same "sorrow" that had overwhelmed her in the mall, with no pride in their union or their home. When they leave the apartment to go to Timmy's, where Anna might feel uplifted, she looks into Sunnycorner and makes a comparison that separates her from the present moment with Wayne. She thinks back on the morning of not making any mistakes in spite of her hangover, and she feels "each step like flight from the apartment" (155). She escapes into the memory of working the cash register, remembering the detailed layout of the store, assisting customers with their purchases, in charge.

What Anna will do is not revealed. She begins the next day "out of habit" (156). The routine of her life is reflected in her rising early in spite of the fact that she has the day off. Her apartment is cold, and she is confronted by the vacuum cleaner and feels "suddenly tired." She retreats by going back to bed, "away from the memory of last night's striving flesh," her sex with Wayne as unfulfilling as her reaction to the new day. Before she gives in to sleep, she remembers their conversation after their failed attempt at making love when Wayne names other things on which they should have spent the money. But Anna knows, "There's too much to get. There's no way we could ever get it all" (157). She retreats in sleep to wake again to the routines of the coming day.

In the final scenes, Anna listens to the stereo, losing herself in song as she had earlier escaped in sleep. With this action, she becomes an accomplice, her participation in the music suggesting that she has accepted her partnership with Wayne or is at least waiting to see how it will turn out. Later, at the Laundromat, as she watches two older women fold clothes at a long table, the question becomes whether she will eventually join them, their connection suggested, as Miner posited, by place, "specifically a working-class woman's place. . . . For the moment, Anna remains somewhat separate from the other women," further noting that, in a few years, Anna will be just like them, her childhood over, and she will be trapped in the confines of her working-class life. For Miner, the "flatness of the story reflects the future flatness of Anna's life" ("Jumping" 23). However, this outcome is only one possibility.

In fact, the final action is ambiguous, and perhaps the uncertainly of the ending reflects the shift that occurred in the middle of writing the story. Dubus discussed the scene in Timmy's after the robbery as a turning point in the writing process: "I realized that they really loved each other. . . . It wasn't supposed to be that. It was supposed to be a betrayal story. I got it out of *The Boston Globe*. A guy robbed a bank; he went to a phone and called his girlfriend in Florida; she said, where are you? He told her; she told her [new] boyfriend, and he called the cops in Boston while she kept him on the phone. So that was why I started ["Anna"]. But in the bar scene I realized that these people loved each other, so, I said, I don't know what the fuck the story's about, and that's when it started to move" (Edenfield 179–80). Anna in fact does love Wayne, and as she sits in the Laundromat, watching her clothes and Wayne's "tossing past . . . like children waving from a ferris wheel," she is waving goodbye to naivety (158). Through the actions of the robbery, Anna has confronted her present life and has seen and been affected by its cheapness. Thomas Kennedy has concurred with this reading, seeing Anna's realization that "acquisitions do not bring the satisfaction they were seeking" as "a note of hope . . . the first step in Anna's self-definition of her existence" (*Andre Dubus* 16). She knows that she cannot be happy with what she has not earned; however, just as she reconciles herself to her discomfort and ends up playing the records and eventually enjoying the music, Anna may readjust her domestic expectations, settling on simply waiting around with Wayne.

Violence shatters the peace that Polly Comeau believes she has found in Dubus's novella "The Pretty Girl," from *The Times Are Never So Bad*. Told from two points of view, the story begins with Raymond, Polly's ex-husband. His first-person narrative is confident in spite of the fact that he has been wounded and is still struggling to understand where he and Polly went wrong. He tells his story directly while Polly's third-person voice is fuzzier, distanced by narration just as she is distanced from herself. While she has only a vague understanding of her place in the world beyond her ability to use her good looks to manipulate men, Raymond lives in a world of absolutes with the energy and determination to make things happen. Strongly built and handsome, Raymond likewise is aware of the power of his body, the way it affects his life and makes negotiations between himself and the rest of the world go more smoothly. On the other hand, Polly is passively contained within her beauty and only superficially participates in her life. Nevertheless, both know how to use their bodies to get what they want in the world. Just as Raymond's large frame gives him autonomy, Polly's power is tied to her beautiful face. When she and her husband split and he cannot reconcile himself to the loss, he punishes her by bringing terror into her life just when she believes she is on the verge of making something happen. Though she wants to create a place of independence, she lacks the imagination to craft such a future. Instead, she falls back into old habits, waiting and making herself attractive enough so that a man will do the work for her.

All her life Polly has been aware of her beauty and its usefulness. She had friends in high school only to have something to do between the boys who made up her real interest. She believed that other girls and, later on, other women did not really like or trust her, that her beauty and her indifference made them jealous. She had only "the friends you need to keep from being alone, and to go to places where boys were" (28). These superficial relationships are actually no different from those she has with every other person in her life. In fact, Polly does not connect with anyone except her father. She sees in her sister a beauty that is wasted, as it is not "the sort that makes men change their lives" (24). Instead, Polly admires the power inherent in her own pretty face, as she can use it to make people act in her stead. Defined by her physical beauty, Polly drifts through life, using her influence over everyone, even the people she claims to love, to give her what she wants.

After Polly graduates from high school and wastes a year proving to her parents that she is a C-minus student not interested in college, she takes a job at a department store and later in her uncle's jewelry store so that she can have money enough for her own apartment. Her days fall into a vacuous routine of work and the beach and going to Timmy's. In the emptiness of her days, Polly is content for a while as no one demands anything of her. Just as she had stayed on the surface rather than engaging in the compositions that she wrote in college, she reaches the conclusion about life that "every topic was difficult if she began to immerse in it; but always she withdrew" (31). Connections take work that Polly is not willing to put forth.

Nevertheless, in a rare moment of introspection, Polly awakens to the discovery that her life has no direction. With superficial values, making no demands of herself beyond her own pretty face, Polly takes stock. Sitting alone in her apartment, she realizes that *"this is the real world they always talked about"* (34). Feeling the emptiness of her days, she is afraid as she sees for the first time that she has done nothing to prepare herself for life. She knows that her routine is shallow, and though wanting "motion, she could not define it, for it had nothing to do with place or even people, but something within herself: a catapult waiting for both release and direction" (34). Though Polly wants to change, to move forward, she has no idea how. Out of habit, Polly attempts to fill the void by attaching herself more permanently to a man. She uses the passive power of her beauty to draw Raymond to her. Drinking alone one afternoon, on the upper deck of a marsh-side bar, she sees Raymond and his friends return from fishing. Recognizing him, she starts to call, then decides to wait. She stands, framed before him: "She wore a white Mexican dress and knew how pretty she looked standing up there with the sun on her face and the sky behind her" (35). Throughout the story, Polly defines herself by her clothing, her power enhanced by her carefully chosen dresses that she knows will attract men. As she predicted, Raymond is taken in by her prettiness and his desire.

The longer he is with her, however, the more he begins to believe that there is something to her other than her good looks, something beneath the surface that is worth loving. When he and Polly go camping one weekend, Raymond watches her domesticate their tent, a temporary space of rented canvas that she transforms into a makeshift home: "The way women turn places into houses, even motel rooms. There are some that don't, but they're not the kind you want to be with for the whole nine yards" (6). Raymond sees the possibilities of a positive marriage in Polly's housekeeping, and for five years they make a life together. Polly feels changed by her marriage, more grounded by the expectations of being a wife with new connections to her community: "She felt both released and received, no longer in the town, a piece of its streets and time, but of the town, having broken free of its gravity" (35). Her marriage at first feels familiar as it comes with the prescribed patterns of behavior that she can simply fall into without having to think what to do on her own.

Though Raymond happily settles down into a predictable life similar to that of his parents, with their daily chores and meals together, Polly soon gets bored. Her life up until her marriage had been defined by her ability to attract and hold a man's attention. Though Raymond is committed to her, the tediousness of their routine starts to weigh on her. Just as she had married Raymond to fill a void in her life, to give her direction, Polly once again turns to a man for diversion. She cheats on Raymond out of boredom, for something to do, "one of the small assortment of choices for a week night" (50). When Raymond finds out about her affair, he beats Polly, who escapes to her parents' house. The way she leaves, sneaking out the back window instead of going through the front door, works metaphorically to suggest her passivity in getting out of the marriage by cheating on Raymond instead of honestly confronting him. She stays with her parents while she begins divorce proceedings, and she and Raymond are never together again except in the continuing violence that connects them.

Incapable of thinking of Polly freely moving around in the world while he is trapped in his misery, Raymond plots revenge. He rapes her in her new apartment and then beats her boyfriend, sending him to the hospital, where he is reduced to a "bruise on a pillow" (22). This attack brings a fear into her life more real than anything she has ever known. Typically able to manipulate men, Polly is helpless against Raymond's unpredictability, so she turns to what she knows, her father, who will do her every wish. He has the male authority that Polly depends on, not just in his physical strength and his love for her, but in his position on the police force, which gives him added power. She transfers her pain to her father and predictably waits for him to make things better. Similarly, he turns to what is familiar: he buys her a gun and teaches her to use it. Dubus saw Polly's relationship to her father as a reason why she did not develop beyond the superficial: "I don't think there's anything wrong with the way [her father] loves her or anything he does to help her, but having his love and approval and having the looks, combined with whatever other elements in her character make her a bit spiritual slovenly. There were no demands. . . . She had what looks like good luck which when combined with her soul was dangerous. That no matter what she did she was loved at home and out on the streets she can make a man fall in love with her. Which in another character could be only blessings" (Edenfield 162). With nothing to prove to herself or her parents,

Polly makes her way by using her gift, her beautiful face, without giving back to the world anything of value. Therefore, with no history of how to perform on her own, no reserve on which to draw, Polly has to turn to a man to protect her from the chaos she has started.

In the few days that Polly is at home with her parents, healing from the rape, she begins to take stock of her life for the second time. Back in the safety of her former home, she has time to think. On most of her afternoons before her marriage, she had spent little time reflecting. When she wanted to relax, she would go to a bar alone, perhaps making conversation or watching people or simply letting her mind drift, empty. In flashbacks of those afternoons or in present-tense descriptions, she is defined by her appearance, the dresses she chooses, the make-up she wears. She is limited by the superficial way in which she sees herself. She is an article of clothing, a skin shade. On past afternoons, she had never thought; rather, her "heart beat faster with a sense of freedom" (30). With nothing on which to reflect but her own pretty face, Polly had been content to sit and attract men. However, confronted by a fear she cannot control, she begins to think, and in her deeper awareness of self, she confronts the vacuity of her life: "There was no single act or even pattern she could isolate and redeem. There was something about her heart, so that now glimpsing herself waiting on tables, sleeping, eating, walking in town on a spring afternoon, buying a summer blouse, she felt that her every action and simplest moments were soiled by an evil she could not name" (39). She simply knows that when she returns home, comparing herself now to her sister, Margaret, there is something about her sibling that she herself does not have. Nevertheless, Margaret's sense of purpose will never be available to Polly, for she does not see the value in her sister's disciplined routine, in her early-morning runs to keep herself strong, in her virginity, in her strong religious faith. Margaret's choices call for deep convictions, a discipline that Polly rejects. Though she wants more in her life than the empty routines into which her days have fallen, she does not know how to change, for "she did not and could not know what about herself she disliked and regretted" (26). She cannot know because she is unwilling to do the hard work that going below the surface requires. Polly goes to Mass every Sunday out of habit, but as with most routines in her life, she makes no spiritual connection. She feels that she lives in sin, though she does not name it, cannot confess it, and so cannot receive communion: "She did not pray with concentration, but she did not think, either, and her mind wandered from the Mass to the faces of people around her" (27). As in her life outside this service, Polly watches, takes in the faces, the physical, not engaged in the spiritual rituals.

As the story progresses, the more frightened Polly becomes, the more she identifies with her father. She bonds with him as he teaches her to shoot with accuracy and confidence, and as she moves into her father's world, preparing herself against potential violence, she begins to feel more in control. When he takes her to get photographed for her gun permit, her shift in perspective becomes evident as she watches the photographer trim her picture, slicing through her breasts: "The black and white face was not angry or hating or fearful or guilty; she did not know what it was but very serious and not pretty" (39). In the shot, Polly sees her colorless self stripped of her former passivity, which had been granted by her beauty. Now, in fact, her looks are what she believes continues to draw Raymond to her, and she feels "dangerous with her slender body and pretty face" (24). When she drinks in Timmy's, she has what she perceives as an added strength, the gun she keeps nestled against the lipstick in her pocketbook, a new addition to her arsenal of power.

When Polly leaves home again, she moves in with Steve, the bartender at Timmy's and the biggest man she knows, as well as the gentlest. Steve's house is the perfect transition; he protects her in her first week out while she takes on the role of wife. The two sleep together "for release from carnal solitude," and for a short while they act as a "couple who have lived long together" (22). She gradually takes over Steve's house, moving into the master bedroom that Steve leaves vacant each summer while he is away on vacation. Polly falls into her predictable behavior with men, using Steve to get what she wants, knowing he will demand nothing of her that she would not willingly give. Polly "begins to feel that more than this one room is hers; not only hers but her: her sense of this seems to spread downward, like sentient love leaving her body to move about the three rooms downstairs, touching, looking, making plans" (55). When she gets the flu as Steve is leaving, she is free to rest in bed and think while seeing herself in motion, walking in the woods, ice skating: "*Do it,* she tells herself" (55). She feels a sense of contentment with her space that reflects a change within herself and the new perspective she has of her possibilities: "This doesn't have to end until it ends on its own, and she can lie here and decorate the house, move furniture from one room to another, one floor to another, bring all her clothes from her parents' house, her dresser and mirror. . . . Tomorrow she will smell trees and the lake" (55). She imagines herself at harmony in her new environment both inside and out. She sees herself walking "in the woods on brown leaves, under yellow and red, and pines and the blue sky of Indian summer" (55). The brilliant colors are beautiful, and this is the peace that Raymond shatters, threatening her in a way she is now trained to defend.

In discussing the novella, Dubus made it clear that Raymond was not coming to attack his wife, not to repeat the rape but to talk, "That's all" (57). When he takes off his clothes, he does not intend for her to see him as a predator. As

Dubus said, "I wish she would have listened to him. He was making sense. . . . If he hadn't drunk, gotten drunk—that did it. She shot him because she thought he was going to rape her. He wasn't going to rape her" (Edenfield 159). Polly sees Raymond as he was, and understandably, she fears him. However, after she shoots him, rather than call an ambulance, she calls her father. Kathryn Nowicki Benzel has attempted to defend Polly, seeing the shooting as Polly's effort to defend her new self, "a woman satisfied in her new identity and responsible for her life" (88). Whether or not Polly believes that Raymond has come to hurt her or not is never clear. Certainly, she shoots him to save what she believes are the possibilities found in her new environment.

The naturalism that Joyce Carol Oates has pointed out in her reviews of Dubus's fiction dominates many of these stories of women who struggle in various ways against destructive forces in their lives. Their homes are backdrops that provide telling metaphors for the negative domestic experiences they must endure. Ineffectualness comes from myriad places. Leslie is frozen, unable to escape her impending death because of the fear and shock that have come to define her days. She is trapped in her home with no power, a cold and dark place that she can escape only through memories of her father. Rose also endures physical violence in part because of self-loathing. Her one moment of action, standing up to her husband and rescuing her children, is not enough to sustain her. Likewise, violence threatens the peaceful home that Polly is trying to build for herself while Juanita and Ruth are equally trapped in their grief for the time to come. However, not all women protagonists in Dubus's stories are determined in negative ways by their environment. Though many of his female characters are temporarily held back or forced to make modifications to deal with crises, many do make the changes necessary to move on with productive lives. Sometimes, this involves breaking from family, even if only temporarily, and four works are tied together in this narrative: "Miranda over the Valley," from *Separate Flights* (1975); "The Fat Girl" and "Adultery," from *Adultery and Other Choices* (1977); and "Molly," from *The Last Worthless Evening* (1986).

In "Miranda over the Valley," Miranda must break free of her parents and her boyfriend, Michaelis, who betray her when she tells them that she is pregnant. When she waits to call to tell them the news, she imagines her parents in their home, their evening ritual so familiar to her that she knows where her mother will sit, what drink will be in her father's hand, the rooms of the house, the pool in shade, the lawn, and finally "those glass doors that one morning when she was twelve she opened and, looking down, saw a small rattlesnake coiled sleeping in the shade on the flagstone inches from her bare feet" (154). The memory works metaphorically to suggest the temptations that await Miranda beyond the protection of her parents' home, where she lives in the "fearful certainty of love" (153). She never expects that her parents and boyfriend will not want to help her keep her baby, that they will not make adjustments to accommodate a new life.

The apartment that Miranda shares with Holly, a friend from home, while she is at school in Boston initially works in contrast with the stability Miranda feels in her California home and with Michaelis. She is repelled by the way Holly cheats on her long-distance boyfriend as she rationalizes her behavior with a flip "nobody owns me" (153). The boy Holly beds is simply marking time: "there was no motion about him" (149). Miranda rejects this static life, and confidently in love, she conjures a kinetic image of carrying her child on her back while she and Michaelis march in protest lines as he wields his law degree as a way to improve the lives of migrant workers. On the evening of her arrival home, where she anticipates putting her daydreams in motion, she first sits alone in the night before joining the others who wait inside. She had seen the look in her mother's eyes "that told her she had been foolish" (154), and the fog that settles around her serves as an imagistic correlative for her sudden uncertainties and the feelings of imminent betrayal. Her spirit of hopefulness for the life that grows inside her is engulfed by her parents' resistance and their influence over Michaelis, who, she realizes, "has not been living well with his fear" (155). His body, turned "slightly away from her" and facing her parents, reveals to her that she is alone in wanting their child. Kennedy has noted that Miranda "sees herself surrounded by people for whom human relationships are a matter of convenience, or pragmatism" (*Andre Dubus* 21). Her father holds a brandy glass but does not drink, as if not partaking can distance him from what his daughter is being asked to do. On the other hand, her mother drinks and only pretends to listen, "hearing again lines she had played to for a hundred nights, and waiting for her cue" (155). She tries to convince her daughter that she will be nothing more than a "dumb little housewife" (156) if she marries without her degree. Michaelis, she imagines, will move on ahead of her daughter: "Out in the world, he'll be growing, and all you'll know is diapers and Gerber's" (156). Her mother cannot imagine beyond her stereotypical conclusions, and her father only wonders, "why suffer," when she does not have to (156). With Michaelis having surrendered to their side of the argument, Miranda recognizes that she has lost not only this argument but, in giving up her baby, she has lost herself, too. She lets go of Michaelis and joins a world of uncertainties.

Perhaps to punish herself, she takes on a lover whom she does not love, feeling "wicked": "Her body was quick and wanton; but her heart was a stone; her heart was a clock; her heart was a watching eye" (162). Her heart knows that this empty sex leaves her feeling divided from herself. At Thanksgiving, when

Miranda goes home with a friend rather than returning to California, she is already on her way to separating herself from her parents and Michaelis. She rejects her parents' materialism just as she refuses their offer of a vacation to Acapulco in return for the abortion. At the end of the story, having returned home for Christmas, she makes love to Michaelis for the last time and admits her infidelity, punishing him for his betrayal by admitting her own. Saying goodbye, she leaves him "naked in the dark" (165), echoing her own vulnerability as she sat in the fog on the night she was betrayed. She will never recover from the loss of her baby, but will find new strength in her independence, leaving her past behind and moving into a "brave new world."[3]

As Miranda has to let go of her mother's view of the world, so, too, does Louise in Dubus's story "The Fat Girl," set in 1960s and '70s Louisiana. The story's narrative focus is Louise's gradual awareness that she is not interested in maintaining the body necessary to please her mother and husband. Her father has always loved her in spite of her plump body, his eyes bathing "her with love" whenever he has looked at her (45). The "bare lunches" she is forced to endure by her tense and rigid mother, who combats her own appetite with cigarettes, are never enough, and Louise's hunger becomes a metaphor for the approval she wants from her mother as well as her classmates. Louise eats candy in secret every day as she rebels against her mother. Elizabeth G. Peck has pointed out that "while being fat has traditionally been equal with being 'out of control,' researchers have more recently recognized fat and compulsive eating as ways of gaining control rather than relinquishing it—despite their personal and social repercussions" (71). When she is alone, Louise knows who she is: "She was fat because she was Louise. Because God had made her that way" (46). However, her mother's disappointment makes her doubt herself.

When she is inspired by her roommate, Carrie, to lose weight, Louise notices a shift in her personality. She becomes nervous and irritable: "In all her life she had never been afflicted by ill temper and she looked upon it now as a demon which, along with hunger, was taking possession of her soul . . . [which] was on some rootless flight. She knew neither its destination nor where it had departed from" (51). She diets to please her roommate and her mother, and for a while she is inspired by their validation and attention: "The new clothes and the photographer made her feel she was going to another country or becoming a citizen of a new one" (54). She marries a man she does not really know but who fits the type for whom she has redone her body. She spends five years before getting pregnant with her son, years that provide her with the "pelf of marriage . . . by slimming her body she had bought into the pleasures of the nation" (55). At times, she feels connected to her house and husband, who has provided her with friends and martial comforts, vacations in Europe, and a life of relative ease. Yet, these moments are brief, as more often she feels as if she had "taken a wrong train and arrived at a place where no one knew her, and where she ought not to be" (55). In fact, her diet suggests that she is starving emotionally, and she goes about the routines of her day without thinking or engaging.

When Louise becomes pregnant, however, she beings to change, eating when she is hungry and providing nourishment for her baby and herself. She comes to love her body "through her son's mouth; while he suckled she stroked his small head and back" (57). In the final scene, Louise leaves the room to shut out her ranting husband, whose conditional love she will learn to live without: "Beneath Richard's voice she hears [her son's] soft crying, feels it in her heart. . . . She brings him to the living room and sits holding him in her lap, pressing him gently against the folds of fat at her waist" (59). In Peck's analysis, "getting fat and staying fat is one way of saying 'no' to gender expectations and sexist restrictions, one way of saying 'no' to powerlessness and self-denial, and one way of refusing to bow to social control" (71). When Richard leaves, she will be free to live without criticism, avoiding a marriage like that of her friend Carrie's parents. Louise "carries the boy to his crib, feels him against her large breasts, feels that his sleeping body touches her soul" (59). She reconnects with herself in her new role as mother. The home she will create for herself and her son will be an empowering place of security, as she will be free to love her boy on her own terms.

In "Molly," Dubus again takes up the issue of women and men who have married only to find that their diverse ideas about home and family are not compatible. Claire and her husband, Norman, separate when their daughter is only three and a half. He had eaten her meals "as a pet dog eats its dry food, out of hunger" but with no relish, no real appetite (118), as he has no passion for his marriage. When he leaves to move across country, his contact is limited to his monthly check, and this financial independence makes Claire free to enjoy her life with Molly and the career she makes for herself once her daughter has grown older. The two meet every evening for tea and drinks to talk before dinner as Claire seeks to connect with her child and "felt blessed, sitting in candlelight, pleasantly well-fed, drinking wine; and oblivious of their soiled plates on the table and the pots waiting in the kitchen to be emptied and cleaned, she sank warmly into the pleasures of motherhood" (124). Molly models herself after her mother, and their deep connection is demonstrated in the metaphorical reference to her singing her mother's songs, the old jazz songs that had played in the background of her childhood, songs with words she did not even know she knew. She takes up her mother's voice, in effect becoming her mother. Lucy Ferriss has referenced a passage by theologian Henri Nouwen: "Becoming the beloved means letting the truth of our Belovedness become enfleshed in everything we think, say, or do" (234). Molly metaphorically celebrates her mother's influences by singing her songs. She rereads her mother's favorite novel. She sees her mother in place of herself in her sexual explorations with Bruce, but gradually she is able to overcome this disturbing image as she begins to connect more fully with the boy she loves. As she and Bruce drive, she stares out the windows at houses and imagines the "routine of their lives—work, habit, or something of the spirit—held them at home as surely as it contained their hopes" (166). She learns to see the world for herself, through her boyfriend's car window, which metaphorically connects her to other Dubus characters whose perspectives are changed by rides in automobiles. A new awareness comes to her when she realizes she is free to create her own history just as she has control over her own future. She will learn to separate her mother's experiences from her own and will move into the "brightness" that "dazzled her eyes, her heart" (177), the brightness of her future.

In "Adultery," Edith has been married eight years when she finally realizes that she must leave her husband, Hank, in order to feel peace in the world again. In the fifth year of their union, she discovers Hank's affairs and that he does not want to live confined to one partner. Bound by her roles as mother and wife, Edith decides to remain in the marriage and meet Hank on his own terms by taking lovers of her own; however, after three years of empty searching, she finds the courage to redefine herself and leave Hank behind. Set up as a frame story, the external narrative takes place over the two days in which Edith decides to leave while the internal action catalogs the details of their eight years together. During their courtship, she uses her money to make herself useful to Hank, serving him good food and drink, dressing up to offer him meals in her nice apartment, providing a routine, cooking while he "stood at the entrance of the alcove, and they talked" (139). Hank stands in a liminal space, framed by the doorway, neither in the room nor out of it, just as he is never quite all the way committed to Edith, though all their habits "felt like marriage" (139). Hank's only "demand was that he write, and that he write well" (138). He breaks down his every day according to his work schedule. Once they marry, he decides that one child is enough, and as he continues to set their parameters, Edith comes to see that "one thing has to be said about men who have found their center; they're sometimes selfish bastards" (142). Hank uses his career, the ritual of his writing, about which he speaks "almost reverently," as an excuse for each of his decisions (140). Her life changes, and while she pretends for three years that she is happy with the marriage that includes her affairs and Hank's, she realizes in the life that she creates with Joe, her current lover, that her ties to Hank must end.

The story opens with Hank and Edith in their kitchen, their daughter sleeping while Edith clears away the dishes, preparing to go to her lover's house to fix him dinner. How she and Joe met is never a focal point of the narrative; instead, what she has meant to Joe and what she has learned from his need have led her to confront the vacuity of her life with Hank. As she has cooked for her lover in his apartment on other evenings, she has rediscovered in herself "what she once felt as a wife, that her certain hands are preparing a gift" (130). In the sacredness of her actions she once again experiences "the sacrament involved in preparing food for a loved one, sustaining the physical body while the love with which she prepares it nurtures the soul of both giver and receiver." She has lost this with Hank. She tries to express her unhappiness, but finds herself "at the dead end of love's grief" (151). She lets go of Hank only to love a man to whom she must learn to say goodbye. Joe's cancer will separate them soon, yet Edith will be able to live in the world without him or Hank, made stronger by her love for Joe, who brought her back to herself, the temple of herself that provided him with an "earth-rooted love . . . for God" (169). In the final frame, Edith awakens at Joe's house on the first and only night she spends there. Later, at the hospital where he will die, she makes the decision to stay with Joe until he passes and to leave Hank behind. She has come to value each day by being made aware of her own mortality through Joe's impending death. She will find healing in a peaceful place that she will create for herself and her daughter.

The ability to move into the world by overcoming momentary setbacks allows Miranda and Louise as well as Molly to move beyond their parents' expectations. Edith must create a more positive life outside her marriage. Each of these women must reject negative ties, redefining their respective spaces or leaving them behind altogether. Imaginative and strong, these four protagonists find happiness by finding love on their own terms.

CHAPTER 4

Fatherhood, Marriage, and *Dancing After Hours*

Andre Dubus wrote with an immediacy brought about by personal experience as he attempted to frame men's roles in the shifting boundaries of domestic space that have, until postmodernism, been fairly consistent. As women have left on journeys of their own, men have stepped into homemaking roles, having to create spaces for themselves in what up to this time has been viewed as a woman's domain. Judith Fryer has focused on the malleability of gender roles as a result of cultural change, referencing sociologist Erving Goffman: "one learns to play a variety of roles by making smooth adjustments of the requirements of social scenes, performances that highlight official values like an ongoing ceremony that comes to be taken for reality itself" (9). Mirroring the shifting political landscape of the 1970s and 1980s, the complex issues of domestic space in Dubus's short stories focus on men and, in extreme cases, exclude women.

Two life-altering institutions dominate Dubus's fiction, two states in which he found himself many times, fatherhood and marriage. He would father six children and marry three times. Four of his six children he shared with his first wife, Pat Dubus, and two girls with Peggy Rambach, his third wife. His marriages and the relationships with his children were the subjects of many interviews, and each one manages to touch on the importance of family. From his earliest story, "The Intruder" (1967), Dubus has been interested in the complex relationships that make up families, and the focus of many of his narratives is on how protagonists are compelled into action by their responsibilities at home. How the characters react to often violent circumstances serves as the framework for many of his stories involving fathers and husbands who, for a variety of reasons, have to renegotiate their connections to their families and their domestic spaces.

Matt Fowler of "Killings" in the 1980 collection *Finding a Girl in America* attempts to bring healing to his family, which has been shattered by tragedy but, in doing so, cuts himself off from any future sense of peace either at home or in the world. Hank Allison, one of the main characters in stories first published in separate collections and later brought together in a three-part cycle in *We Don't Live Here Anymore* (1984), loses his family because of his selfish attention to his career and his unwillingness to live within the compromising limits of husband and father. For a while, his best friend and colleague, Jack Linhart, goes along with Hank's so-called logic about open marriages, but Jack eventually realizes that the bond he has with his wife and children is too tight to break and that he will never leave them. Hank, on the other hand, is eventually betrayed by a woman he thought he loved, a woman who aborted his child without his knowledge. When he finds out, he is devastated, yet he is eventually healed by his connection to his daughter, Sharon, and the young woman, Lori, to whom he has pledged his heart. Likewise, though Luke Ripley of "A Father's Story" from the 1983 collection *The Times Are Never So Bad* is rocked by his daughter's accident, he immediately responds to what he claims to be the rights of a father toward his child. He defends her by covering up her crime, and he lives with it by justifying his actions to God. "The Winter Father" from *Finding a Girl in America* (1980) deals with failure and successes as Peter Jackman learns to build a new home for his children in the wake of his divorce.

Dubus's last collection of fiction, the 1996 short-story cycle *Dancing After Hours,* brings together the most nurturing view of home. Beginning with LuAnn's graduation from college and moving into her work world of empty routines, she eventually progresses into marriage and motherhood, where she manages to succeed in both roles while losing herself in neither. In the final LuAnn story, "Out of the Snow," she defends herself against her attackers, the violent scene in her kitchen becoming a metaphor for her fight against the various forces throughout her life that have threatened to overwhelm her. The cycle celebrates a woman who is able to create a space for herself worth defending, a life that neither overwhelms nor disempowers her. The satellite stories that surround the LuAnn and Ted narratives add to its domestic themes. Each one works to support the cycle's movement toward healing, of recovering from the violence of ordinary living. In the final story, "Dancing After Hours," Emily is on her way to being healed; the story and, consequently, the cycle end with two people reaching out to one another with promise.

Within the confines of their domesticity, Dubus's male protagonists struggle to find their places as roles shift and families either break apart or come together, depending upon each character's ability to reconcile himself to the conflict in his life. While some are able to create positive environments for both themselves and their children, others are held back by their inability to come to terms with a particular crisis. In his efforts to recover, Matt Fowler of "Killings" destroys any hope of ever being at home in the world again. He lost his youngest "in a way no father expected to lose his son, and he felt that all the fears he had borne while they were growing up, and all of the grief he had been afraid of, had backed up like a huge wave and struck him on the beach and swept him out to sea" (10). Cut off from his formerly peaceful life, Matt decides to seek revenge against his son's killer in an effort to bring comfort to his wife. In doing so, he embarks on a journey that creates an irreparable divide between the couple.

Matt had always been a protective father who worried about his children's safety. When the three were small, he would watch fearfully as his two sons and daughter would play in the snow, climb trees, and swim in the ocean. Always, Matt was aware of the possibilities of accidents, of death taking one of his children from him. He was "relieved when he came home in the evenings and they were there" (10). However, not wanting to transfer his fear, Matt would watch without warning, careful not to make them afraid. He and Ruth are welcoming to Frank's girlfriend in spite of her violent ex-husband. Perhaps the same protective nature that so defines Matt also influences Frank, who is a lifeguard after all, to want to protect Mary Ann, whose small frame carries the weight of single-mothering two boys. Matt hopes that his son will "soothe the pain in her heart, take it from her eyes" (9). This pattern of responsibility, of wanting to bring peace and comfort to a woman in need, later prompts Matt to act out of character in devastating ways.

After burying her son, Ruth retreats to her home, staying shut up with her pain. When Matt and his friend secretly decide to kill Richard to offer Ruth some sort of comfort, Matt faces his victim in his personal space, and the photograph and neatly made bed, the tidy living room—all the details of Richard's home—make Matt, a father and husband, too, aware of the enormity of his actions: "He was conscious of the circles of love he was touching with the hand that held the revolver" (14). This killer is a son and father, a lover to someone. Richard is brought into focus for Matt, who had been blinded by despair to the consequences of his actions. Yet he does not look Richard in the face; instead, he keeps focused on the gun, telling Richard lies to keep him packing. To keep himself motivated, he reminds himself of Frank, seeing him alive and happy, sitting on the couch with Mary Ann's boys, "feeling loved, hearing Mary Ann moving about in the kitchen." The nurturing scene is enhanced by Mary Ann's entering with sandwiches, nourishing her family and "smiling at [Frank], saying something the way that women do when they offer food as a gift" (13). Remembering this sacrament of love that Richard destroyed gives Matt the courage to force the young man into the woods. In a reaction to Richard's attempt to flee, Matt shoots him in the head: "The gun kicked in Matt's hand, and the explosion of the shot surrounded him, isolated him in a nimbus of sound that cut him off from all his time, all his history" (18). In killing Richard, Matt is reduced to the same level as his son's murderer. Dubus concurred: "He doesn't gain his life; he does something terrible. . . . At the resounding of the pistol shot, I think at that moment he knew that he had forever violated nature and he would never be in harmony with it. He has broken his own harmony with nature; he is isolated forever" (Edenfield 173). Though Matt had tried to convince himself that killing Richard would make sense of the chaos, he ends up causing even more grief: to himself, to his wife, and to his children, who must live with the belief that their brother's killer got away. As Dubus pointed out, "now the lies are compounded, and it's just worse and worse. . . . To commit a cold-blooded murder, you'd have to believe that you could get away with it. You have to believe there is no spiritual life. No God. No victim to live with. And you have to have something deeply cold in you. Matt doesn't have that. Revenge and hatred and protection of children all feel very normal until you actually pull the trigger and kill somebody. It's not something that Matt Fowler can do with peace" (Edenfield 173). Matt's actions will not help his wife. When she reaches for her husband in the final scene, offering herself to him, he cannot make love to her. He cannot bring himself to share his pain and "shudders with a sob he kept silent in his heart" (20). Matt will not be able to reconnect because of his inability to confess his regret.

On the other hand, although Luke Ripley of "A Father's Story" also breaks the law, which may have resulted in a young man's death, he is resigned to his actions, which he takes in defense of his daughter. In fact, at the end of the story, Luke not only reconciles himself to his crime, but expects God to understand and accept without judgment as well. He relies on rituals, as other protagonists do, drawing on various acts of meaningful repetition. This pattern of responses has contributed to Dubus's established reputation as a Catholic writer. By his own admission, Dubus has been defined by his faith. "I am a Catholic writer," he told Susan Larson in 1991. "I always look for 'what's the ethical question here?'" (Edenfield 131). His childhood friend, Vaughn Simpson, made it clear in a 2013 interview with this author that his religion was central to his work: "I don't think you can understand his stories at all unless you understand that fundamental Catholic root of what he does." His oldest sister,

Kathryn, during the same conversation would agree, pointing out the importance of his "Catholic worldview." Vaughn finished, "You cannot take him out of the mentality of the Catholic environment."

This Catholic framework enriched Dubus's life, transforming the ordinary events of his every day into sacred acts of spiritual awareness, were he only present in the moment to witness. As Dubus told Eleanor Wachtel, the rituals of the Catholic sacraments are "physical transactions with a spiritual meaning" (Edenfield 139), and for many of Dubus's characters, their reactions to conflicts, choices made in defense of those they love, become sacred rituals of faith against dark forces at work in the world. The accidents, the crimes, the acts of betrayal by those beloved—the myriad reactions to these various events are hinged to rituals of faith, sacraments of love born of an abiding concern for family and one's roles and responsibilities. As Suzanne Hunter Brown has rightfully concluded, "such rituals can separate the secular and divine or merge the two" (232).

As Luke did, Dubus turned to rituals of faith after his accident, leaning on his devotion to Christ and his example as he learned to live with the frustrating disability that robbed him of his physical energy and temporarily stole his ability to write fiction: "If it weren't for prayer, I'd be fucked," he told Stacey Chase in an interview following the accident. "When you grow up with the Passion of Christ as an example, I mean, you know at least there's a membership of suffering. And you get the focus that you're not the only one in the world who's got things rough" (Edenfield 107). In the years of recovery, Dubus took communion daily. He told Tim McCarthy in an interview that in the spring of 1998 he swooned when "the Eucharist minister anointed him at home. He would lie there on the bed with his eyes closed, unable to move. And sometimes he had visions of Mary. . . . Another time she hugged him and he felt really loved" (Edenfield 126). All the visions were tactile, sensual. Rightfully, then, the earliest studies of Dubus's work emphasize the spiritual overtones of his stories and the influence of the Catholic Church. As Regina Hackett wrote of Dubus's protagonists, "They argue with God. Sometimes they allow themselves to be moved by His grace and sometimes they pass it up, conscious of what they are doing" (Edenfield 118). God is a real and present force in their lives. Sometimes, however, his characters make deliberate choices that seem, at first, to contrast all that has previously defined them. Oftentimes, as with Luke Ripley, Dubus's most debated protagonist, they go on to justify their actions, perhaps in the name of love. They stand on fresh principles defined by new ways of seeing themselves as they adjust to shifting roles and responsibilities.

In the morning ritual that Luke establishes, he is able to move through the guilt of covering up his, but, more important, his daughter's crime. Daily, he makes his case to God, confirming that his actions, born out of a father's love for his daughter, are not merely right, but sacred. In fact, at the end of the story, Luke not only reconciles himself to his crime but also expects God to understand and accept without judgment. After covering up Jennifer's accident, he admits that he does "not feel the peace I once did; not with God, or the earth, or anyone on it," yet he goes on to say that he "has begun to prefer this state, to remember with fondness the other one as a period of peace I neither earned nor deserved" (179). Prior to the night of his daughter's accident, he knew that his life might have appeared to be only what people saw from the outside: a divorced father of grown children making a fairly good living providing riding lessons and boarding horses. Yet he knew that his real life went on beneath the surface of what people could witness, that the deep meaning of his days came in his connection with God. Through the action of the story, Luke expands his previously tranquil, though solitary life by stepping into the role of Jennifer's protector, acknowledging this new self in his concluding explanation to God.

Luke's family left him years ago, and the peace he was living in prior to Jennifer's accident had been difficult for him to achieve. He created new rituals against the silence of the lonely mornings, waking to spend an hour in meditation with God: "I offer Him my day, every act of my body and spirit, my thoughts and moods, as a prayer of thanksgiving, a habit from boyhood in a Catholic school; or then it was a habit, but as I kept it and grew older it became a ritual" (162). This routine helped Luke work through his first months alone, and in the present action of the story, years after everyone but Jennifer, now twenty and in college, is already independent, Luke continues to rise each morning "feeling the day, in silence" (163). As he readies himself to go into the world, Luke fortifies himself with the rituals of his faith and with the blessings of each new day.

Much of the story is given to Luke's reflections on his life prior to and immediately following his actions on the night Jennifer wakes him to tell him that she has hit someone with her car. Gradually, he had learned to redefine his life, to live in peace with solitude, content finally with the discovery that it "is not hard to live through a day, if you can live through a moment" (167). He gave himself over to routines, believing in the healing power of action elevated to ritual. Receiving the Eucharist each morning, he felt "excitement" and "spreading out from it . . . the peace of certainty" (165). Luke transcends the ordinary habits of praying and receiving and confessing to establish a deep connection with God. Luke thinks, "Ritual allows those who cannot will themselves out of the secular to perform the spiritual, as dancing allows the tongue-tied man a ceremony of love" (165). Faith's ability to justify action with love likewise validates Luke's cover-up of Jennifer's crime. When he breaks the secular law, lying to the police as well as to Father Paul, Luke responds to a higher calling that redefines him: "for when she knocked on my door, then called me, she woke what had flowed dormant in my blood since her birth, so that what rose from the bed was not a stable owner or a Catholic or any other Luke Ripley I had lived with for a long time, but the father of a girl" (179). From that defining moment, Luke acts out of his new role as his daughter's protector.

Though he had always been a part of Jennifer's life, enjoying the summer months and vacations she would spend with him, he had up until that evening felt separated by their genders. Now it is the very difference of their genders that Luke feels justifies his actions and binds him to his child. For Thomas Kennedy, this is a "story about the demands of moral action and moral principle weighed against the even greater demands of love, parental love, specifically the love of a father for a daughter" (*Andre Dubus* 75). Luke again has to redefine his place in the world, which up until Jennifer's accident had been an extension of the spiritual connection he had at church, set into motion each day in his morning meditations.

Though he will never feel that peace he had prior to the cover-up, he prefers this new role, which connects him more fully to Jennifer. He feels neither "loneliness nor shame, but as though [God] were watching [him] . . . as I have watched my sons," he thinks, "at times in their young lives when I was able to judge but without anger, and so kept silent while they, in the agony of their youth, decided how they must act; or found reasons after their actions, for what they had done" (179). Just as Luke witnessed and understood his sons' struggles, he knows that God understands him and offers gifts in exchange for what is lost. As Kennedy concluded, Luke's "action was a movement from that awful solitude of the heart toward the fulfillment of his destiny as a parent" (*Andre Dubus* 76). Jennifer looks her father "full in the face as I had never seen her look, as perhaps she never had, being for so long a daughter on visits (or so it seemed to me and still does: that until then our eyes had never seriously met)" (176–77). This emphasis on perception—of truly bringing the other into focus—corresponds with Luke's new way of seeing himself as this girl's father, and the connection that he feels from and for his child will sustain him just as, metaphorically, it is Luke's love behind his actions that transubstantiates what would otherwise be a crime into an act of love.

In the final scene of the story, Luke explains to God why he risks his hard-earned tranquility. Sitting at his window, watching the day come into focus, Luke continues his rituals of giving thanks, talking to God: "Of course, He has never spoken to me, but that is not something that I require. Nor does He need to. I know Him, as I know the part of myself that knows Him, that felt Him watching from the wind and the night as I kneeled over the dying boy"

(179). He knows that God has witnessed his crime, but that He has also seen his heart, the love that in sacrifice transforms his actions. In this, he is reminded of another sacrifice. He knows that God "would not lift the cup" of suffering from his own son, just as he, like God, "could bear the pain of watching and knowing my sons' pain, could bear it with pride as they took the whip and nails" (180). Yet the final argument that he makes to God crystalizes his new role: "But You never had a daughter," Luke reminds God, "and if You had, You could not have borne her passion" (180). Through his sacrifice, Luke receives a stronger connection to Jennifer that marks him for another calling. By risking everything for his daughter, Luke experiences sacramental love. He justifies his actions to himself and to God, taking on his and his child's sin as an obligation of fatherhood, which, for him, overrides conflicting laws and commandments alike.

Dubus confessed to Wachtel that he was a "tender-hearted father towards daughters, much more protective [than he was with his boys]. . . . I'm not saying that's good or bad; I'm just saying that's the way it is" (Edenfield 135). Yet, as he told John Smolens, Luke's decision in regard to Jennifer would not have been his own: "I would *never* do such a thing as cover up for a hit-and-run accident for one of my daughters, and none of them would ever ask me to do that. So I never said that what Luke Ripley did is good. I think the character's good, but he's wrong" (Edenfield 213). Nevertheless, Luke would respectfully disagree and sees his fatherly actions as holy.

Just as Luke had to struggle to find his place when his marriage ended, so, too, does Peter Jackman of "The Winter Father," collected in *Finding a Girl in America*. The newly divorced father works to create a positive place for his children and himself. Though he and his wife had both left the marriage vows years before, twelve years have passed before the two decide to divorce. Afterward, Kathi and David live with their mother while Jack gets the children on the weekends and every Wednesday night for dinner. Through the action of the story, which takes place during the winter and early months of summer, he and his children learn to live together again. When Jack brings his eight-year-old son and his six-year-old daughter home to his apartment for the first time, he understands the difficulty of maintaining intimacy with his children, a connection he has in the past taken for granted. His new apartment is made up of "empty rooms," and when he returns home, he feels "as though with stooped shoulders, he were limping. . . . He wondered if he looked like a man who had survived an accident which had killed others" (110). Spiritually and emotionally wounded, Peter is afraid that his vulnerability will spread to his children, making the break-up of their family even sadder and more confusing.

Going to pick up Kathi and David from his former home, Peter feels physically connected to the landscape: "Already the snow-plowed streets and country roads leading to their house felt like parts of his body: intestines, lung, heart-fiber lying from his door to theirs" (111). He wants his children to feel a connection to his new apartment as well as to their former space. To make everyone feel comfortable and to create a sense of intimacy, they fix a meal. As the three cut and wash and mix, the familiar motions of cooking both ensure a good memory and distract them from the difference of their father's new home. As Peter performs the rituals, he is aware of "a presence to his rear, watching, listening. It was the wall, it was fatherhood, it was himself" (112). Peter wants so badly for his children to feel at home that he is conscious of his every move. His tentativeness is understandable as only his children's happiness can absolve him of the guilt of leaving home. As long as the three are busy with their kitchen tasks, they work in harmony. Only when they stop and sit down to their meal do they become aware of "the white silence coming at them. . . . the kitchen was multiplied by silence, the apartment's walls grew longer, the floors wider, the ceilings higher" (113). Their new dwelling seems to grow in its unfamiliarity.

The story begins in winter, at the start of the new year. Metaphorically, this calendar suggests the Jackmans' new start as each family member begins not only a new year, but a new way of living, the parents now separated by a forty-five-minute drive. The car ride reminds the children of their family's break-up: "Now their talk was the same, but it did not feel the same. They talked in his car and in places he took them, and the car and each place would not let them forget they were there because of divorce" (119). He wants a space where his children feel as if they are "together as a family" (128). Only when they are able to go to the beach with the return of summer does Peter feel fully connected. Their makeshift home of blanket, cooler, and umbrella provides them with an unrestricted place where no one feels awkward; rather, it "was the place they wandered back to: for food, for drink, for rest, their talk as casual as between children and father arriving, through separate doors, at the kitchen sink for water, the refrigerator for an orange. Then one left for the surf; another slept in the sun, lips stained with grape juice" (128). On the blanket, the family becomes a unit again through the autonomous movement of each individual. They have the liberty to move, returning to the blanket for sustenance, which metaphorically suggests a sacramental ritual as sacred as the receiving of Christ's blood and body. In the final scene of the story, the children are rejoined to their father both physically and spiritually, holding his hands as they nap in the sun on either side. This peace of summer with its symbolically hopeful light will, should things turn out for the best, transfer to the winter apartment that awaits them, longing to be called home.

While fatherhood is a recurring focus of Dubus's stories, the marriage theme likewise appears in all his collections. Several characters bind three of the collections. Through the first two stories of the three-part short-story cycle, Hank Allison appears to be a man who cannot be happy in a monogamous relationship. When Edith asks Hank to leave at the end of "Adultery," he spends the next four years in affairs, primarily with students, young girls who want no more from the relationship than he does. However, when he learns in "Finding a Girl in America" that his former lover had aborted his child a year prior, Hank is affected enough by this loss of potential life that he finally takes stock. He gradually begins to see his faults in his marriage to Edith. With this new perspective, he can start again with Lori, a girl whom he has come to love.

However, before Hank reaches this level of commitment, he spends years defined by a selfish attention to work. His best friend and colleague, Jack Linhart, tells Hank's story as well as his own in "We Don't Live Here Anymore," first collected in *Separate Flights* (1975). Jack makes the point that he is "surrounded by painful marriages that no one understands" except for his friend Hank (13). He has lost interest in his wife and takes on Hank's philosophy regarding home: "You live with a wife, around a wife, not through her" (26). He belittles his wife, Terry, whose faults he observes and catalogues and thumbs through for the conviction to leave. He distrusts the limited self-awareness he sees in the majority of men around him, and both he and Hank congratulate themselves on their own understanding of the complications of life. Jack criticizes his wife's extra weight and their messy house, judging her by her failures, focusing on what she does not do rather than all that she does: "It was living that defeated Terry," he decides, "the rooms where we slept and ate and the living room and dishes and our clothes" (47). He sees her in terms of her home. He even sees his wife's weight gain as a betrayal, a broken promise that she would not get fat; each of the eleven extra pounds is a testament to her dishonesty. Making love to Edith or simply spending time with her, he justifies his deception by imagining his wife moving about their house in her daily domestic defeat: "Trying to plan her work for the day overwhelms her; it is too much" (9). He concludes that his house is a metaphor for his marriage, "dirty," and that just as his children return home every day "hungry," he also craves more (9). Nevertheless, his guilt at what he is doing to his family is clear in the way that he tries to compensate by bringing home their favorite foods that he cannot afford, luxuries like lobster and fixings for banana splits. Still, he feels stifled in his home and carries an image of his wife in a new dress: from "her scheming heart his balls hung like a trophy taken in battle from a young hero long dead" (42). Jack feels trapped by Terry, held captive by his responsibilities to her. In Jack's fantasy, a wife stands in a kitchen with "bright curtains and walls" that suggest a clean home. However, the house that Terry keeps is always one step ahead of her, and rather than pitch in, Jack judges her, sees her as so connected to the house that its very dirtiness is a reflection of her character. This anger and manufactured sense of neglect provide him with the excuse he needs to justify his affair with Edith.

In spite of her own frustrations, Terry speaks up for herself, reminding Jack, "I don't keep a Goddamn Howard Johnson's for you, because I read a lot and, you know, think a lot" (58), She won't let herself be defined by what she knows are sloppy housekeeping skills. While Jack can say that Terry has broken a promise by putting on weight, her responsibilities at home have also interfered with her returning to her job. Now the only career she has are chores she loathes. Her lack of engagement in the daily cleaning tasks is in essence a refusal to be defined by what she sees as a limiting role. "I read somewhere that booze and suicide claim many of us, us housewives; did you know that? No other group in the country goes so often to the bottle and the sleeping pill" (58). After his wife's directness, Jack is finally honest with himself and his children, a moment that comes when he takes his children sledding in the park the next morning. When he looks down into their questioning faces, he tells the truth, unable to lie to his son and daughter though he has been pretending and lying to himself in an effort to justify his affair with Edith, the lovely housewife of his fantasy, who cooks well and maintains an orderly house. She is all that Terry struggles to be and each day plans to be. "Your mother and I love each other," he tells his children. "She's a good and wonderful woman, and don't worry about anything you heard last night, people are all sorts of things, and one mistake is only a small part of a person." He has begun to see that Terry is more than her house, more than dust and dirty floors: "I stood alive again and breathed the rain-scented air and I knew that I would grow old with Terry" (68). He recommits himself in that symbolic moment, the water anointing the family and blessing their new start.

That the Linharts as a couple have promise is seen in the contrasting outings that occur in the final scenes of the first and third stories of the cycle. In the first, though the children beg their mother to join them in the park when their father takes them sledding, Terry pulls back, staying home. However, in the final scene of "Finding a Girl in America," all four are brought together on their beach blanket spread for their family. As Dubus himself summed up to Kennedy, "those who are willing to experience the pain of love . . . will experience joy and that is always better than emptiness" (*Andre Dubus* 97). Their physical placement is evidence of the strength of Jack's commitment to stay with his wife and to work to regain a genuine commitment to her. Again, the scene takes place near water, a healing symbol and a hopeful space that suggests promise for the couple.

For Hank, progression and understanding come more slowly, and he undergoes a series of meaningless affairs until he is made to evaluate himself and his past actions by the grief that he feels over his former girlfriend's abortion. Although Monica gets rid of the baby before Hank even knows she is pregnant, he blames the conception on his reckless sexual behavior. He has been divorced from Edith for four years when "Finding a Girl in America" opens. He has remained close to his daughter, whom he respects and loves. He is careful of her feelings, yet is frightened by her maturing body. He fears that the lack of commitment in his life is setting a bad example for Sharon, who knows of his father's many girlfriends. Hank wants to change, to commit to Lori, who gets along with his daughter, and now watching the two together, "he feels, in the empty chair beside him, the daughter salined or vacuumed from Monica a year ago" (160). Hank is wounded by this loss, and the sadness changes him, makes him more aware of Sharon's maturing. He wants more for his daughter than a series of temporary relationships built on little more than sex, as many of his past relationships have been. As he starts to consider others besides himself, he arrives at a fuller and more meaningful understanding of love, which leaves him accountable for his past actions: "Forgive me," he asks Edith, for "everything" (166). His atonement and Edith's forgiveness lead him down the path toward forgiving himself. As evidence of his change, he brings Lori into a part of his life that he has heretofore only shared with his closest male friends. On one particular afternoon, though the two would typically have gone Dutch, Hank provides the meal, his picnic working in contrast with the older man's dinner that Hank had spoiled in the first story. He promises to court Lori and to marry her if she'll have him: "No more playing with semen and womb if getting pregnant means solitude and death instead of living" (182). He commits to Lori and plans a life with her at the halfway mark of the running trail. Earlier on, Hank had noted that he had reached the midpoint of his life. Now, halfway on the trail just as he is halfway to death, he makes a new commitment to life through his love for Lori. The way home is downhill. "It'll be quicker, going back" (183), he tells her, just as their life together will hurry past in the peace of belonging.

The majority of the male characters in Dubus's short fiction have autonomy, and the choices they make bring them to various crossroads. Characters such as Hank and Jack risk everything, bringing pain into their lives and the lives of their families. Peter Jackman likewise has suffered through a divorce that has caused his family members to have to redefine and reshape themselves as they grow used to his being away. Matt has moved far from the peace he once knew. His home can no longer provide him with its former comfort, and he isolates himself within his remorse. Luke Ripley, though he is secure in his decision to protect Jennifer, will never again feel the peace he had worked so hard to achieve. Luke justifies his actions to himself and to God, taking on the sin as he takes on his new responsibilities. These myriad challenges facing Dubus's male protagonists are evident in other works. His only attempt at a detective story, the novella "Land Where My Fathers Died," is a whodunit, the result of a father's fury over his teenage daughter's affair with a doctor who preys on her negative self-image. Dubus's fathers are typically protectors, and their absence from family can fall hard on sons, as evidenced by "The New Boy," whose protagonist, fourteen-year-old Walter, having just begun to awaken sexually, feels the immense responsibilities of being the only male in a house with two sisters and a mother. Their sexual activity confusingly excites and angers him, and he wants both to protect and punish them. Likewise, in "Bless Me, Father," Dubus illustrates yet again the complex relationships between fathers and daughters. The binding ties of fatherhood unify his collections. Men take stock of their lives in relation to their children and take action in response to those commitments.

His final collection of fiction, the short-story cycle *Dancing After Hours* (1996), is an appropriate ending to a career that celebrates the healing power of the human heart in connection with another. In the LuAnn and Ted stories, each character reaches a place of peace after years of struggling to find ground. Both have been wounded by love; however, they meet and marry, building a happy home together and later having children. The satellite stories, beginning with "The Intruder" and ending with the title story, "Dancing After Hours," work to reinforce the movement toward healing, opening with a young boy's violent and damaging defense of his home and concluding with a mature woman's determination to trust in love again. These stories in tandem encapsulate Dubus's career, which began with the publication of "The Intruder" in 1963 and closed with the same revelation in *Dancing After Hours* that many of his fellow short-story writers would make, a "recognition" of the "emptiness of a life that turns away from human contact and the possibilities of love" (Kennedy, "The First and Last Stories" 230). Kerstin W. Shands has noted that during the 1990s, escape imagery was pushed "out of rooms and out to boundaries and borderlands, accelerating the movement metaphor to hypertransgressive speeds, while at the same time celebrating metaphors of flatness, dissolution, and instability" (11). While some of Dubus's characters expand the borders or move away from the protection of home and family, an equal number draw tight circles around their domestic spaces. Shands asked whether it is not "possible for a sense of place to be progressive; not self-enclosing and defensive, but outward looking" (147). In fact, this cycle ends by answering this very question and standing testament to the possibilities of love and home.

"The Intruder" has been dealt with in chapter 2, and just as the home is more than backdrop in the opening story, it is equally significant in the second of the satellite stories, "A Love Song," in which Catherine is irrecoverably wounded by her husband's infidelity. The pain of his request for a divorce is compounded by his having brought it to her while seated at the table in their kitchen, where for sixteen years she has cared for her family. She is left without foundation: "The earth itself was leaving with her sad and pitying husband, was drawing away from her. Stars fell. That was a song, and music would never again be lovely; it was gone with the shattering stars and coldly dying moon, the trees of such mortal green; gone with light itself" (21). The world has shifted in her perspective and only after a long struggle does she find herself able to look outside the window to where nature has restored itself, the green grass and blue sky beyond her casements mirroring a tendency that Shands has seen in feminism's "exploration of spaces and boundaries" that "in many ways duplicates postmodernism's similar positing of structures, spaces, and boundaries to be collapsed, displaced, or transgressed" (17). Little by little Catherine's home is restored to her as she plants a garden, tilling the soil to bring comfort to herself. She chooses a partner who makes no demands on her. In contrast to her home, his apartment "was not a place where someone lived; he ate and slept there. . . . his home was like an ill-kept motel" (26). While she celebrates her daughters' marriages with hopefulness, metaphorically, however, she will not venture over her property line nor invite anyone in to stay. She is content within herself.

Perhaps Catherine's unwillingness to connect is due to the pain she still feels over her divorce. Certainly, loss motivates the female protagonists of the next two satellite stories, "Blessings" and "Sunday Morning." Both stories take place early in the morning following two very different but catalytic events. In "Blessings" Rusty is the mother of two grown children and the wife of Cal, a man with whom she has lived happily without threat or fear save for a few weeks of worry when her daughter had pneumonia. Prior to Gina's illness, Rusty had found herself blissfully "awake and alert" (44) to her life in the evenings when her family was home. Even moving through her solitary days, Rusty—her husband's name for her—speaks to her mate as if he were there, going through her routines with her. She is no longer Margaret, her parents' child, but Cal's wife and mother to their children.

The present action of the story takes place one year after the family has survived the sinking of their chartered fishing boat, an accident that killed both crew members. The family has rented a lake cabin, and while the rest sleep, Rusty wakes in the dawn, then sits on the porch and waits for her sleeping pill to work, imagining herself walking "back through the house, into bed and sleep," all the while battling the "cluttered" memories of the accident (69). These are soothed by a metaphorical moment in nature: "She looked at the doe backing away from the water, raising her head; then Rusty saw the length of [the buck's] body emerge from the woods, as if he were growing out of the trees, just fast enough for her to see. At the lake he stopped, his head up, listening. Then he drank" (69). While one drinks, the other stands guard, and what works in nature works as well for Cal and Rusty, whose family has managed to survive. The rented cabin further reinforces the temporariness of living, an awareness that becomes for Rusty a blessing as she once again takes stock of her family. Kennedy noted that the final story ends with a "recognition of mortality" ("The First and Last Stories" 230). Indeed, each of the satellite stories makes reference to death, and part of the progression of the cycle is a movement toward characters who recognize the blessings in each day as they are conscious that they stand in the face of an ever-present threat to lose it all, a threat that Dubus knew well.

Awareness of death can go another way, too, as it does for Tess in "Sunday Morning." Tess has lived daily with the fear that she will "grow old and die alone" (73). She has longed for a husband and child, but with each passing day she feels that time has become her enemy. Her biggest threat to finding a partner, however, is not time but her inability to put into perspective the fate of a friend who was murdered by her husband. The violent death took place in her friend's new home, and the story has stuck with Tess. She is driven to tell it with an urgency and anger that has frightened away her former lovers. Even now, telling Kenneth, she looks at his eyes and "could see flight like birds" (81). This satellite story, coming midway in the progression toward healings, effectively jars any simplistic views of postmodern relationships. Tess will remain alone, reliving her friend's death, which makes her fearful of marriage. She lives alone in a cell-like apartment, so small there is no room for a kitchen table, and lets her fear of death affect the possibilities that life might offer. The allusion to the Wallace Stevens poem with the same title reinforces Tess's yearning for permanence. However, fear of death severs her from the more meaningful life she so desires.

This is the realization that the poet's dying brother longs for his sister to reach in "Woman on a Plane." He has come to a place in his illness that has dissolved his fear, leaving only "goodness itself, as though death were stripping him of all that was dark and base, mean and vain, not only in him but in the world, too, in its parts that touched his life (100–101). For the first time, she resents the pull of her job, which keeps her from being with her brother, and she wants to know what he knows, the peace that passes understanding, which she sees in his dying eyes: "She wanted it while her body was strong, while she was vibrant and pretty" (102). Though she is afraid of flying, she no longer wants to be afraid of living. Waking in her apartment alone every day, she gathers her "scattered self" to face the uncertainties" (102), to pull herself in from hurt to a restorative faith, much as Robert Townsend of "The Colonel's Wife" must do.

Townsend's accident has left him broken and in intense pain. While he is recovering, he is trapped in his house, through which he can no longer navigate. Until his accident, home was a refuge from his duties as a marine colonel. His infidelities while he was on tour were kept secret from his wife, and he lived with certainty while he was home and, when away, always imagined his wife in relation to their house: "He had never had any feelings about the things of domestic life. In them he saw Lydia's choices, and his admiration was not for the objects but for her" (109). Now, with his limited mobility, he is kept from both his dining room table and from his wife's bed, though he has no appetite for food or for the body. His hospital bed provides him with a view from the dining room window, where the acres that surround their house comfort him. His bed is "narrow" (104), his grief immense. He grows fearful of fire, a metaphor for what he knows has been extinguished in his marriage, fearful that, were an accident to occur while he was alone, he would not be able to escape.

A change in the colonel begins when he starts to notice the value in the objects of home. He starts to see the pieces of furniture and the walls of the house as ballasts against the shifts that occur in life. Looking through the window, where he gets a broad view of his land—his life—the table that he looks past stands as a testament to his marriage to Lydia, which had "traveled in moving vans back and forth across the nation. . . . . He had lived with it for decades, and now, lying helpless and in pain, he began to feel affection for the table. In the mornings he opened his eyes to it; at night in the dark he looked at its shape in the pale light of the window" (109). The table has withstood the movements of their lives, has been the centerpiece of their meals, and the reminder of his absences as well. As he begins to appreciate his home, he begins to value his wife: "He liked this new way of seeing the house, as if the entire structure were female and he entered it to be at its center with Lydia; and she had made a place for him, his den, as she gave him a place in her body" (112). He feels "tenderness" toward his wife and closer to her at the same time that he suspects her of an affair, seeing in her eyes "something that was not in the room, some image or memory" (115). Broken by his accident, he cannot face the breakup of his marriage, and he lives through the first afternoon of his suspicion in quiet fear. When he awakens, fitfully, from a nap, he cannot locate Lydia in the house, and the grief that follows is intense and cathartic. When she holds him, he knows that she "loved him; and if he had never known precisely where she was, she had finally always been here" (119). His own infidelities quiet his condemning hers, and they lie on the bed and make plans for their future, remodeling the house and widening the doors, moving the top floor to the ground, giving access to all the rooms that were now only his wife's. He tells her, "I'm glad that damned horse fell on me. It made me lie still in one place and look at you" (121). In the images of sunlight illuminating the room, hope radiates and displaces the darkness of his earlier nightmare. They will move to Arizona to her family's lake house while their own is being rebuilt, made new as their marriage is made over in his newfound appreciation of his "golden-haired wife" (103).

Robert Townsend eventually recognizes what has yet to come to Lee Trambate of "The Lover." At fifty-five with three ex-wives, he is still searching for the absolute that he believes love to be but which has not found him, and "always [love's] ending had flung him into a dark pit of finitude, whose walls seeped despair as palpable as the rain" (133). He spends most of the time alone, writing in his small apartment. His solitude drives him to fantasies of his three wives and all of their children living together under one roof. His need for his family is so great that he cries over his loss to a young woman with whom he temporarily connects: "Where do I go for that? What street is it on? Where's the door?" (137). He is the lover, not husband or father, but a temporary man. This story contrasts with the one that follows, "The Last Moon," which is told through the perspective of a woman who has grown so bored with her marriage that she manipulates one of her high school students with whom she is having an affair into killing her husband. This ripped-from-the-headlines tale follows a predictable plot, but the point of view coming from the woman adds to its effectiveness. Like other characters in the cycle, she is defined by her associations to her home. She distinctly remembers the day when she and her husband bought their house and furniture, though she has moved so far away from her commitment to him that "she did not feel the bed holding her, or the room, the dead witness of its wall; she felt only her body" (140). She plays house with her husband, but does not feel at home, as the only real life goes on inside her body, in her physical self, "in that place where she now lived" (143). She believes that her husband's death will provide her with the money for escape that will take her "through the night sky, her thumb and forefinger open to hold the moon" (144). Yet, as the title reveals, this view will be her last of the moon. Widowed by choice and rejecting her home, she makes a mockery of the fear of loss suffered throughout her marriage by the unnamed protagonist of "At Night," the story that follows.

Even as a young girl, the narrator had seen herself in a "house alone, with photographs of children and grandchildren on a mantel over the fire" (169). She imagines a long illness for her husband and dreads his pain and the suffering she fears will one day come for him. Her own death is immaterial to her, for "here she was each morning, with him" (170). Most of the three-page story is given to the details of their life together, the years after his retirement when they eat together, walk together, "and they went to the children and grandchildren, and the children and grandchildren came to them, and there was the house to keep, and the cooking, and their garden, and friends for a visit" (170). They live happily with a routine that unites them as a couple until death comes for her husband in his seventy-seventh year: "her love went out of her, into his cooling skin, and she wept for what it had done to him, crept up and taken him while he slept and dreamed." She imagines his spirit "wandering" and "maybe confused," seeing her still there, "lying beside his flesh, touching his cheek, saying 'oh hon—'" (171). Even in death, she sees her husband with her, his concern for her grounding him there in the room as she confronts both his loss and what he has lost. Having imagined his death every day for half a century, she has been aware daily of the temporal nature of life, an understanding that enriched every minute of her marriage and then would act to intensify its loss.

Death fills the pages of *Dancing After Hours.* Nevertheless, in spite of its portent, or because of it, many of the stories radiate with desire, of protagonists who wish to connect with life in defining ways. Each story deals with a character searching, reshaping or redefining his or her place in the world. The satellite stories are particularly effective in moving the cycle to a positive place of healing. Space and one's relationship to home is a binding theme as is the journey toward embracing one's place in the world, both of which are enhanced by each story's placement. "The Intruder" and "A Love Song" are followed by the first of the Ted Briggs stories. In "Falling in Love," Ted, too, is betrayed by his lover just as Kenneth feels betrayed by his sister and just as Catherine has had to learn to adjust to life without her husband. Ted's pain is intensified by his story coming on the heels of these characters' similar conflicts. Likewise, LuAnn's need in "All the Time in the World" to move beyond the temporary moments of connection with her job and her boyfriends is in part enhanced by the two stories prior. Like Tess, LuAnn is aware of time passing without her having made a meaningful life for herself, and like Rusty, she desires the peace of protective partnership. The placement of the narratives emphasizes how easily such seemingly simple desires can be stripped away or never allowed to come to fruition. Rusty has to learn to trust again, to believe her family can withstand the world's dangers. This, too, is LuAnn's charge when she first meets Ted, who literally and metaphorically helps her find her footing and starts her on her journey toward home.

Ted Briggs in "Falling in Love" has come back from Vietnam physically wounded. He walks with a cane, an injury that makes him feel conspicuous. He feels outside of his community, generally comprising people who did not support the war nor his involvement in it. His girlfriend, Susan, a woman who defines herself by her work, is drawn to Ted perhaps for his resilience, his ability to survive war with only a slight limp and need for a cane, as much as she is for his wide chest and strong frame: "She liked the strength in his arms hugging her" (31). She feels his embrace more permanently than the "fullness" she experiences with acting, a three-day high that would leave her feeling "arid and lost" (29). This description is hauntingly portentous of the post-abortion emotions that Ted suffers when Susan decides to terminate her pregnancy rather than carry their child to term, in spite of Ted's promise to raise their baby himself. He grieves for lost life and for the possibilities of love that he is aware may pass him by—the same thoughts that worry LuAnn in the ironically titled story "All the Time in the World." Each knows that time is precious, and each is conscious of how much has been wasted.

As in many of Dubus's stories, homes are used in reference to characters and their various relationships to themselves, others, and their place in the larger world. LuAnn's parents' house, where she still has a bedroom, makes her "feel that, since graduation from college, only time and the age of her body had advanced, while she had stood on one plane, repeating the words and actions she regarded as her life" (90). She enjoys her job but has no interest in becoming like her boss, a woman who spoke of money "with love, even passion" (86). Likewise, her previous partners have seen family as "something that might happen" one day (87), each one talking about "marriage as a young and untried soldier might talk of war" (88). The reference to war and the ability to survive it sets up her meeting with Ted, who is the opposite of those lovers from her past who seem now to LuAnn to live life on the surface. Ted is a tried soldier, wounded by war as well as by love, who, like LuAnn, is ready now for a home and family. As George Lakoff and Mark Johnson have pointed out, human beings "are all containers with surfaces and 'an in-out orientation'" (Shands 38). Ted and LuAnn meet with the simultaneous desire to be filled by another, and when they connect, they are able to let go of their urgency regarding time as they begin to prepare their life together. Ted tells her, "I want a home with love in it, with a woman and children" (95), and LuAnn sees him as a "gift" (96). Her focus grows more positive at work, for she does not try "to plunder from an empty cave a treasure for her soul" (97). She simply wants more in her life than a career and anticipates the blessings that she knows are coming to her through loving Ted. When she goes to lunch with her friends in the final scene of the story, she orders a large meal, waiting "for all that was coming to her, from her body, from the earth, from radiant angels poised in the air she breathed" (97). She receives the blessings and moves into a space of eternal communion where "there was no time" (97).

The final Ted and LuAnn stories as well as the final, title story bring positive closure to a journey that begins with married characters unable to resist affairs to those who sustain or restructure relationships or who make positive new ones. Some are successful in rebuilding a strong framework. Others are too fractured to recover from loss. Death and divorce add to postmodern concerns not unlike those faced in the earliest American tales, and as the short story evolved, the motif of domestic space provided a consistent reminder of the dangers present in the landscape and the importance of getting one's house in order. When LuAnn makes the conscious decision to refrain from an affair in "The Timing of Sin," she demonstrates the power of free will. In the days after almost slipping into infidelity, she becomes conscious of her life. She makes love often with Ted, and in the mornings she is aware of each of her children. She takes in the smell of the trees, the woods that surround her as she drives with her friend in the early afternoon to play tennis. She notices the houses and imagines living in one: "She loved her life and she knew she would love it in that yellow house, too" (148). She appreciates the solidity of the members of her family's connection to one another, and though she knows they would be a family wherever they were under whatever circumstances, she loves her "big house on the country road and she loved being in it, and was grateful for the money they had" (148). Realizing the blessings of her life, she is thankful for her family. That she defines people in reference to their homes is seen when she imagines the first settlers who also used the road on which her friend's car now travels. She thinks of the wagons and carriages they had driven along dirt roads and of the houses they had built long distances apart. Then, when she compares herself to her friend who has to work, she appreciates that she can stay home to make a comfortable place for her husband and children. For her, people are more fully illuminated in relation to their domestic space.

LuAnn has no need or desire to labor for money though she gives her time to help people temporarily displaced: those who cannot afford homes and teenage girls who can no longer live with their own families. She donates her money and time to young women scattered by misfortune, helping them find more permanent shelters against the dangers in the world that have driven them there. By comparison, she recognizes how lucky she and her family have been. Each story prior to "Out of the Snow" sets up the potential for betrayal on some level. As the stories progress, they build toward the possibility of healing. "At Night," the story immediately preceding it, is a brief reminder that love is worth any fear of loss that comes with it. Risking everything for a moment awakens LuAnn into a new appreciation of her family's need as well as her own.

LuAnn's marriage is saved by her definition of herself in relation to her home. What stops her in the car with Roger in the few seconds that they pull away from each other is the image of herself walking into her house. LuAnn tells her friend, "I saw myself walking through the kitchen and the dining room to Ted in the living room. I didn't see Ted. Or Julia and Elizabeth and Sam in their beds. I saw my face and the front of my body, walking toward—me. Walking on the floor toward me. And I knew I must not do this" (165). She stops, accepting both the blame of moving toward temptation as well as the blessing of the vision that prompts her to stop: herself framed within her own walls. As Shands has pointed out, because "rest has had oppressive or limiting associations . . . and because the essence of feminism has been seen as change, movement-as-change has, not surprisingly, been unquestionably promoted" (4–5). Nevertheless, for LuAnn and for the most peaceful of Dubus's characters, fulfillment comes in being able to withstand the temptations that threaten one's home and remaining in place to face whatever changes may come. Confronted by herself, LuAnn is given a view of what makes her life meaningful, herself within her home, and she confirms what Shands has seen as hope for postmodern troubles: "The significance of place, likened to individual development and embracing both the present and the past family history, suggests that it is only when we accept our family roots and our need for a home that we can find a place in society and move into a more liberating and promising future" (110). LuAnn believes that she was rescued by God, who gave her a vision that led to a final understanding that fortifies her in the horrifying confrontation in her final story, "Out of the Snow," which takes place one year after "The Timing of Sin." In this new awareness of her own personal strength in relation to her family, her home gives her the strength to defend herself.

Each day as LuAnn rises, she defines herself by her place in her family, taking stock of her space, watching her husband move about their bedroom, feeling the quiet of the morning as her children sleep: "it was as though she heard their breath and saw their faces on pillows" (172). In each action of the day, she makes herself conscious as she focuses "on the present now, as she went downstairs, aware of her breathing, her leg muscles, the smell of coffee, the electric light in the dining room and twilight in the living room" (174). In this between time, she pays attention to her movements, cataloging every detail of making breakfast while letting her mind move into the future, where she ponders secure scenes of comfort: Ted safely in Baltimore, eating a satisfying meal; her children in bed. Her will for her family to be safe is as real to her as the pull of nicotine, a temptation she tries to resist as she attempts to ward off apprehension, though there is "so much to fear" (178). Her happiness comes with the awareness that she could lose everything, a fear that eventually she is grateful for: "I started thanking God for this fear, because it meant I love [my family] so much. . . . I looked at that beauty around me, and I was grateful. I was still afraid, but the worst of it went out of me" (178). LuAnn works through her trepidation over Ted's plane flight just as she had earlier taken in the snow and pines; she moves from room to room in her house, straightening and smoothing, stopping for moments at a time to look out her windows at the landscape beyond. She finds a security in her home that comes with the rituals of her day.

All that LuAnn has to lose is set up in the opening scenes of the story. The security she now feels is the reward of her journey that started the day Ted helped her find her footing on that Sunday morning years before. The two had gone to eat together, and images of nourishment, both physical and spiritual, were enhanced by the metaphorical connections to food, the buying and preparing and serving of meals. Food as always became "part of the earth she and Ted would eat. Now that she was gathering food for Julia and Elizabeth and Sam, too, she saw it in the store as something that would become her children's flesh. As a girl she had learned about the seven sacraments of the Catholic Church, all of them but one administered by a priest; the woman and man gave each other the sacrament of matrimony. Being a mother had taught her that sacraments were her work, and their number were infinite" (181). The simple tasks of her day transcend the routine and become rituals as sacred as those of the church. She sees the blessings of her life in the daily work of her days, and in this awareness is the blessing of peace with her place in the world.

Perhaps because LuAnn has such a heightened awareness of her environment, when she leaves the grocery store she is alert to the potential for death that surrounds her. The snow brings with it a feeling of apprehension that she recognizes as the "old and faint dread that was always a part of her thrill when she saw falling snow, as though her flesh were born or conceived with its ancestors' knowledge that this windblown white silence could entrap and freeze and kill" (182). The dark winter setting works metaphorically to contextualize the violence that soon follows. In spite of her usually intuitive self, however, she misses for a moment the cause of her unease. This is not a typical reaction to snow but an unconscious awareness of an evil that would like to destroy her if it could. She soon confronts this evil in the eyes of a young man who reduces her to a commodity, looking her over as if "he were deciding whether to buy her": a new fear settles over her for which she is "ashamed," but she is "angry," too (184). These emotions ride home with her as she takes in the scenery as well as the car in her rearview mirror, a perfect contrasting metaphor for the earlier drive. At the same time, however, this scene mirrors her previous fear that the peacefulness of her present life would be shattered by some outside danger. The metaphorical significance of the rearview, of the danger framed in her car's mirror, is complicated. On the one hand, the automobile has typically served as a place of freedom for Dubus's protagonists, a symbol of escape and of agency, an image of power in the American canon. LuAnn's car, however, is filled with an image of danger, a fear from the past that personifies all of her worry, trailing her now.

In her resolve, LuAnn wins. Rather than surrendering, she faces the accomplices in her home, using her kitchen as an arsenal against the threat she has always dreaded, taking up first a teakettle, then a skillet, and finally the phone after she beats the intruders into submission. Though LuAnn's attackers flee, she follows, memorizing the plates on their stolen car. Though the thieves are never apprehended and though she never sees them again, they remain "part of her life" (189). They stand in her memory as testament to her strength and courage and determination to live: "They collided with me; all this harmony I work for; this life of the spirit with the flesh. They walked into my kitchen and I said *No, God; not like this,* and I beat them with a skillet" (192). LuAnn sees in her power to ward off these men a quelling of the myriad fears that have permeated her life up until this point. She understands now that her place on earth is grounded in her role as mother and wife while she recognizes as well that she fought equally to save herself. She tells her husband, "I didn't hit those men so I could be alive for the children, or for you. I hit them so my blood would stay in my body; so I could keep breathing" (193). At first, she speaks with a tone of confession, as if her actions make her part of that self-same evil she had overpowered. The final action of the story, however, reveals a more redemptive answer as the two sit next to one another: their "legs touched, their hips, their arms" (193), and this connection will not dissolve when the moment passes. Both have come in out of the snow, as the title suggests, and are now peacefully at home, blessed by their understanding of life's temporal yet permanent nature.

These same lessons are those that Emily Moore learns in the final story, "Dancing After Hours." At forty years of age, she is tired of living alone and has grown bored by her habit of turning fearfully away from life. She lives in an apartment where she simply goes through the motions of her days without connecting to anyone. Though she finds pleasure in the routine of her job as a bartender in a Massachusetts town, she came to the work primarily because of the pain of not being able to bond with the high school students she had struggled for years to teach. She had given up and had "taught without confidence or hope, and felt like a woman standing at a roadside, reading poems aloud into the wind as cars filled with teenagers went speeding by" (210). She sees her students seeking movement as a way to flee the limitations of their age, and in turn, by her static nature, she feels isolated from them. Now she works in a bar with no windows, closed off from the world as well as her coworkers and customers. Though always pleasant and productive, she keeps a part of herself hidden, no windows to her soul. As Kennedy has pointed out, the bar is "a kind of limbo and a place of inner as opposed to external vision, a place where people go to numb with drink, music, and company their consciousness of mortality and the faltering of their capacities to experience human love" ("First and Last Stories" 229). Emily makes only small, though kind gestures of connection toward those she serves. She listens to Rita talk about her breakup, asking her questions to show her concern; she is conscious of Kay's crush on Rita and hopes that the waitress will not be rejected and hurt; she worries about her boss, Jeff, and wonders how he manages in the aftermath of his divorce, which a year prior sent him into a mysterious world of loneliness. She goes to extra lengths to see that Drew and Alvin, two visitors who stay until closing, are given the best service: chilling their glasses, she anticipates their needs. Going through the motions of running an efficient bar, Emily focuses on each of her actions, using kinetics to ground her in the moment so as to forget her fear of her future.

She has a habit of predictable routines at home as well, keeping a neat place, shopping for and cooking healthy food. She has order in her small apartment and spends an hour every day walking, connecting to her surroundings. Underneath these comforting habits, however, Emily recognizes that her life is unfulfilling, that she is lonely. All the things that sustain her body and soul "became what she could see and hear, smell and taste and touch; like and dislike; think about and talk about" (203). She feels empty, knowing that "she would never bear and love children; that tomorrow would require of her the same strength and rituals of today . . . [or] sorrow would consume her" (203). Typical of Dubus's fiction, the opening paragraph sets up the conflict. Emily leaves the tasks of her well-run bar to step outside the windowless space into the sun, catching its last light before it sets. Emily, too, wants to step outside of her isolation into the symbolic light of renewing love, which she "longed for but was able to keep her longing muted till late at night when she lay reading in bed, and it was trumpets, drums, French horns; and when she woke at noon, its sound in her soul was a distant fast train" (210). The passion of jazz brings out her desires; however, like the faraway train, like the former students she imagined rushing past her in their cars, she fears that her chance at enduring love has passed her by.

Perhaps because her own home is lonely, she imagines her associates in their living spaces. She thinks of Rita's learning to live alone again, her "walking into her apartment, listening to her telephone messages, standing at the machine, her heart beating with hope and dread; then putting a potato in the oven, taking off her shoes, turning on the television, to bring light and sound, faces and bodies into the room" (203). She projects the same empty coping routines of her life onto Rita, and Jeff, too, who she notices tries to make a life for himself at his job as a way to survive the breakup of his twenty-plus-year marriage. At the bar, he makes connections with customers by meeting their needs, cooking their steaks and hamburgers, “potatoes and clams or fish in the fryers,” making “sandwiches and salads,” feeling brief moments of calm in the routine of preparing and serving good food (205). Emily and Jeff are connected in their complementary actions of serving others. Each uses routines to nourish themselves and others, both body and spirit, but both need to learn from Drew the riches that come from engaging fearlessly with life.

In the scene in which Drew is introduced, he is described three times as smiling. He is a man who has made peace with his limitations by resisting unnecessary restrictions. When he dove blindly, faithfully, into the sea that broke him, he was later mended in spirit when he leapt from a plane, a leap of courage no different, really, from the leap he makes every day, a leap of faith that comes with learning how, good-naturedly, to depend completely upon another. Emily responds to this good man’s willingness to face each new challenge. Rising every day in cheerful spirits, he meets the day, helped along in his rituals by Alvin. Emily is amazed by the joy in Drew’s skydiving story, a jump that shattered his legs. She sees in his fearlessness that, worried too much about the consequences of a painful fall, she has been cheating herself of the highs that life can offer.

Emily’s jump comes when she takes Jeff’s hand and dances with him, connecting through the rhythms of the music, their bodies pressed together. She gives into his lead, trusting him: “He turned her up and dipped—she was leaning backward and only his arms kept her balanced” (226). Her movements match those of Drew skydiving, and like Drew she frees herself to what awaits as Jeff “pull[s] her up close and [holds] her” (226). As they dance, he talks about fishing, about losing himself in the water and sun. Bearing home the catch to clean and cook brings the good feelings of the ocean back into his own environment, if only temporarily. Like Emily, he has found a routine to get him through his days. As he shares, Emily becomes aware of the music, and as the two dance, they are brought together in a new harmony as later when she sings: “Time hurries by, we’re here / And gone” (228). Metaphorically removing herself from her protective space behind the bar, she joins Jeff at the table. She serves him, sits with him, their arms and legs touching in an echo of Ted and LuAnn’s connection in “Out of the Snow.” Emily and Jeff close down the bar with a promise for the next day.

Rather than waking to a Sunday of empty, meaningless routines, the two decide to cook bluefish for lunch at Jeff’s and make plans to fish together on Monday. The moments of connection through dancing and drinking and eating have opened them to one another. As they leave the bar, they find beauty in the night sky, which contradicts the reference to T. S. Eliot's *The Waste Land*. Their future is ripe with potential as they open their doors to each other. Jeff plans to grill on his balcony, which extends from his kitchen, a metaphor for the expansive, nurturing hope that awaits the couple. In Kennedy's view, the two are "transported . . . from a state of emotional shutdown to one where real human contact again becomes possible" ("First and Last Stories" 229). Their hands touch before they say goodnight, and Emily drives east into the dawn of her new life.

Dubus wrote many of his best works about family, about various characters' responsibilities to those at home, and perhaps his own failed marriages made him alert to such problems. Each of the works focusing on family and parental responsibility is unique, the author's range far reaching. "Dancing After Hours" brings positive closure to Dubus's last short-story cycle, which works to suggest what the majority of his characters in all of his earlier fiction had struggled to understand with varying degrees of success. Though they risk being hurt by numerous gambles, those characters willing to trust in the power of human connection can build fortresses that allow for spiritual growth. Some struggle within the home against the very people who have promised to nurture or provide. Others fall into affairs or grow addicted to their work. Yet, whatever unfavorable influences befall these characters, Dubus's fiction, enhanced by the motif of domestic space, ultimately ends with healing promises and restorative images of love.

CHAPTER 5

The Essays

After his accident, which cost him his ability to walk, as well as his third marriage and the daily joys of life with his two young daughters, Andre Dubus struggled, too, with his ability to write fiction. As he admitted to many interviewers and in the essays he turned to as a way to regain his voice, he could no longer identify with his former protagonists, many of whose conflicts seemed inconsequential in comparison with his own. "These days," he wrote in the 1986 essay "After Twenty Years," "I barely have the heart, the will, to do something as insignificant as writing fiction" (*Broken Vessels* 86). Nevertheless, encouraged by his family and friends and by writers such as Tim O'Brien, who visited him many times after his accident at his home in Haverhill, Massachusetts, Dubus began again. The will to write returned primarily from writing essays, which allowed him to confront the many conflicts he was then struggling to overcome in a more personal and immediate way than fiction could ever provide. The forty-seven essays collected in two volumes provide a mirror not just to the author's daily triumphs and defeats but also reflect the themes and truths that abide in his short-story collections. The essays, read in tandem with his fiction, tie together issues of faith and family that are woven throughout his canon. His nonfiction provides another way of understanding Andre Dubus.

Dubus wrote essays throughout his career, and the best of these published prior to his accident in the summer of 1986 have been reprinted in the 1991 *Broken Vessels*. The foreword, written by his friend and fellow writer Tobias Wolff, as well as the recognition he received when the collection was honored as one of two finalists for the Pulitzer Prize in Nonfiction in 1992, adds to this claim. In 1998 Dubus published a second collection of essays, *Meditations from a*

Moveable Chair. Both works demonstrate the writer's wide range of interests, and each essay provides a lens through which to come to terms with his fiction.

Dubus wrote frankly in both collections about the writing process along with the frustrations of marketing short stories to publishers more interested in their own profit than in his prose. As an essayist, Dubus wrote honestly and brilliantly about the daily struggles and triumphs of simply being alive. These are the same themes that consistently appear in his novels and short stories. Close to a dozen of the collected essays touch on his accident, one recounting with painful specifics the night he was hit by a car. The joys of childhood and the hard-learned lessons brought home to a sensitive, perceptive Lafayette, Louisiana, boy; the healing gifts and ties of civilian and military friendship balanced against the prescriptive rules and regulations that might drive a good man to suicide; fatherhood and the awesome responsibilities of nurturing another's soul; the blessings of the sacraments; love and loss—these are the refrains of Andre Dubus, and their melodies resound through stories and essays alike.

Dubus willingly discussed his creative process with many interviewers over the years, and his essays, like the interviews, are interesting for their revelations of the tenacity and courage involved in being a writer of short fiction. The third title in *Broken Vessels,* "Under the Lights," which he dedicated to friend and fellow lover of baseball, Philip Spitzer, whom Dubus referred to as "the brother I never had by blood" (*Broken Vessels* 140), can be read as an allegory for the writer who refused to quit in spite of never reaching the majors and the literary agent who always believed in him. As Spitzer wrote in *Andre Dubus: Tributes,* edited by Donald Anderson, "When I read the manuscript *Separate Flights,* I considered it the best work of fiction I had read in many years . . . [though] we realized our decision to work together tantamount to exchanging a vow of poverty" (106–7). As a boy, Dubus had read and taken to heart Joe DiMaggio's advice to ballplayers to leave the profession if they spent more than one season in Class D or C ball. Writing as an adult, however, Dubus had survived countless setbacks and disappointments; in his essay "Under the Lights," he wrote, "Perhaps DiMaggio wrote the word *quit.* I can't. I've spent most of my life in angry dread of that word" (22–23). For most of his career, Dubus, like the Lafayette baseball players he admired during his boyhood, had a small but faithful following. Dedicating the essay to his agent is fitting as, allegorically speaking, when Dubus writes about the Bulls' first baseman Billy Joe Barrett, he might be referencing Spitzer's faith in him: "with the hope that is the essence of belief, I told myself that he would play in the major leagues" (25). Dubus wrote with grace, just as Barrett played, "his whole body and his whole mind and his whole heart . . . in absolute harmony" (27). For Spitzer, this harmony of heart and mind was the definition of his friend's skill, and he admired Dubus's "courage to stand by his convictions." After losing his friend to heart failure, Spitzer would write, "To this day, if ever I am faced with a dilemma of a moral or ethical nature, I ask myself, what would Andre want me to do" (Anderson, *Tributes* 107). In a sense, he might be speaking of the way Dubus approached his characters, most of whom confront life-changing moments that draw on inner reserves, and while some fail, betraying themselves and others, all do so without judgment.

"Selling Stories" and the essay that follows, "Marketing," from *Broken Vessels,* recount the years spent trying to convince various publishing houses to print his first collection of stories. Dubus served as his own agent for years. Alone, he faced letters of rejection and endured disappointing meetings, all the while tempted by offers of the money that would surely come if he would write a novel rather than the short stories he was repeatedly told would never sell, would not make him or any publishing house any money. Two essays, one from each collection, are tributes to Richard Yates, who taught fiction at the University of Iowa when Dubus was an MFA student in the 1960s. "A Salute to Mr. Yates," in *Broken Vessels,* and "Goodbye to Mr. Yates," collected in *Meditations from a Moveable Chair,* illuminate his respect for Yates and the lessons of fidelity he learned from his mentor. In "A Salute to Mr. Yates," Dubus recounted each sacred detail of his friend's writing space as well as the rituals of the act of composition: "It was, I believed—and still do—a place that should have been left intact when Dick moved, a place young writers should be able to go to, and sit in, and ask themselves whether or not their commitment to writing had enough heart to live, thirty years later, as Dick did: with time his only luxury, and absolute honesty one of his few rewards" (94).

This honesty has been remarked on by Dubus's critics as well, his insistence on telling the truth as he saw it no matter how unpleasant that might be. He reiterates this point in "Selling Stories," which insists on a writer's need to maintain his standards in the face of temptation, to resist giving in to editors' demands just to be able to afford the gold pens advertised on the pages of their magazines. The essay is a veiled allusion to Judas and the silver that bought his soul. How easy to change a comma, to delete a word, to buff out a scene's dirty spots. Dubus, however, would never betray his readers, choosing to publish with the quarterlies that paid him very little, knowing that he would be able to face himself the next time he sat down to write and that his stories would live "alone" on pages "untouched by paper genitals, diamonds, and gold," pure (103). He writes with fairness, even compassion, of representatives from publishing houses who with kind faces and voices of encouragement still had to refuse to publish his first collection, denying him something he admitted to wanting since he was eighteen years old. One woman in particular he remembers for the "long and passionate" letters they exchanged about writing, a woman who wished to accept what he had to offer but ultimately could not grant him the contract he desired because of her responsibilities to her publishing house: "Like doomed adulterous lovers, we could only share our passion and futility and the wish that our lives had not come to this impasse," the "affair" ending after a summer of "hope" (105–6). Rather than promise a novel he did not want to have to deliver, he counted his blessings and kept "his dignity," and with "hope stronger than [his] belief" (109), he eventually found Philip Spitzer, who in turn found David R. Godine, men more interested in art than profit.

These essays about marketing his stories seem on the surface to be merely a recounting of the difficulties of staying true to one's craft. They are in fact tied to the same rules of discipline and honor that he learned in the military, specifically on board the navy ship where he was given temporary command of his marine detachment. These events are fictionalized in his first novel, *The Lieutenant,* but are recounted as fact in "Mailer at the Algonquin," as he remembers "something whose elements were injustice, hypocrisy, and my first confrontation with a bureaucrat; a man who used a swivel chair and the passive voice, and precedents and rules and procedures, to turn away from the lonely complexity of the human heart" (63). The protagonist of *The Lieutenant* confronts and defeats the same temptations to sell out to protect his career that Dubus faces at the Algonquin, where, in exchange for his "integrity" (71), he is asked to rewrite his novel to insure its profitability. These sorts of men and women populate his fiction, and his collections are filled with the quiet triumphs of those who refuse to surrender their dignity as well as the lifelong sufferings of those who do. The essay "First Books" confirms the writer's need to remain true to his code, to "strive to be a better human being than the writer normally is . . . to do this through concentration on a single word, and then another, and another. This is splendid work, as worthy and demanding as any, and the will and resilience to do it are good for the writer's soul" (162–63). Dubus the writer, similar to his best protagonists, confronts the day-to-day moments shielded by sacred principles. As Tobias Wolff observes in his preface to *Broken Vessels,* "the real possibility of the personal essay . . . is to catch oneself in the act of being human. That means a willingness to surrender for a time our pose of unshakable rectitude, and to admit that we are, despite our best intentions, subject to all manner of doubt and weakness and foolish wanting" (xiii–iv). While Dubus was steadfast in his writing and in the marketing of his work, his essays reveal with the same honesty as his fiction the pain inherent in self-betrayal and denial of the beloved.

These are lessons Dubus learned at an early age. His love of Christ and his teachings were at odds with the injustices he witnessed either in his own life or in the lives of those he loved. Always conscious of the privileges inherent in being a middle-class white American male, he used his position to speak up for those who lacked voice. Several of the essays are reminiscent of his stories that illustrate discrimination on the part of the justice system toward those without power, those who are victims of their biology or their environment. "Imperiled Men" recounts the same discrimination in the military against homosexuals that Dubus confronted in his short story "The Dark Men." Just as the fictionalized investigators come to arrest a navy man for charges of sexual misconduct, the commander of the Air Group on board the USS *Ranger* during Dubus's service in the Western Pacific also committed suicide rather than surrender to the authorities. While Dubus gives his fictionalized protagonist the chance to take flight once again, to give himself to the sea in a private act of goodbye, CAG, as his men affectionately call him, dies publically, brutally, eventually bleeding to death from a self-inflicted gunshot wound. He leaves behind men who "mourn," who "would have followed him into hell" to "perish in their brilliant passion," just as CAG has died for his own (44). Desperation comes to the best of Dubus's characters, those pieced together from memory and those created from whole cloth.

"The Judge and Other Snakes" tells of Jan, a high school girl, who was physically beaten in public by a boy twice her weight and then mentally defeated by a judge too arrogant, too intent on technicalities, to hear her case. Dubus lamented, "We have not made a country where there is a lot of room for Jan and people like her to breathe. I believe the judge threw out the case because Jan was a girl . . . and because the judge is old, and tired of people and their continual pain before his bench, and because Jan is not, as the phrase goes, from a prominent family. I will never believe that if her family were wealthy he would have done to her what he did" (74). The judge's evilness is set up by the title's allusion, and the young woman's poverty renders her as powerless in court as she was against the boy's fists, her loss of innocence irrevocable. The essay closes with Dubus going home from the courtroom exhausted from the injustice he has witnessed, the "early dark of winter" a metaphorical indictment of gender and class inequities.

This sort of violence against women was not impersonal for Dubus. His oldest daughter, Suzanne, was for a time trapped in a violent marriage, a situation that her father drew on for the short story "Leslie in California." In December 1991, his oldest sister, Kathryn, was raped by a man who threatened her with a knife in her own backyard, a life-altering moment for her that her brother sought to come to terms with in the essay "about Kathryn," which opens *Meditations from a Moveable Chair.* Kathryn refused to be a victim, refused the stigma felt by many women who are violated. Instead, she told her brother, and as his essay movingly recounts, she kept telling her attacker during the rape, "God bless you. . . . I prayed for him Sunday, at Mass" (6). Dubus recounts the story without sensationalizing, without taking from his sister the dignity that she deserves, though his love for her and the pain he felt at what she had suffered are intensely expressed: "This is my sister who . . . gave her blessing to the man who came with a knife out of the darkness" (9). Her brother's skill at capturing such a terrifying moment with truth and grace is simply further confirmation of Dubus's ability to write sympathetically from a woman's point of view without a trace of paternalism, true for both his essays and his fiction.

The ability to sympathize with others accounts in part for his ability to bring his characters into immediate and sharp focus. "I don't go in as a judge. I go in to become, and if I can't become, it doesn't work," Dubus would answer when one of his characters was criticized in an interview (Edenfield 163). Perhaps this lack of moral condemnation came from his deep Catholic faith, a belief that he, too, had been forgiven for his transgressions and therefore could write without judgment. At least a dozen of the collected essays include references to grace, to being watched over by a wise and benevolent creator who had long ago forgiven his shortcomings. The essay that opens *Broken Vessels* demonstrates exactly that.

In the mid-1960s, Dubus lived with his first wife, Pat, and their four children "in a very old house in southern New Hampshire" (3). So begins "Out Like a Lamb," the first entry in *Broken Vessels:*

> This was my first encounter with sheep. When I was a boy, sheep had certain meanings: in the Western movies, sheep herders interfered with the hero's cattle, or the villain's ideas about his grazing rights interfered with the hero's struggle to raise his sheep. And Christ had called us his flock, his sheep; there were pictures of him holding a lamb in his arms. His face was tender and loving, and I grew up with a sense of those feelings, of being a source of them: we were sweet and loveable sheep. But after a few weeks in that New Hampshire house, I saw that Christ's analogy meant something entirely different. We were stupid helpless brutes, and without constant watching, we would foolishly destroy ourselves.

When the sheep that the Dubus family is hired to watch escape again and again from the safety of their pens, venturing out to create problems for themselves and their keepers, one by one, the caretakers lose their patience and begin to retaliate, in spite of their knowing that the animals have no malice in their hearts and "did not want to leave their pasture, at least not for long and not to go very far" (4).

This analogy is carefully set up. Just as the sheep stray, so, too, does everyone, and though Andre Dubus's God can forgive and forgive, more often than not the tendency he observed in humans is to retaliate. We are not "sweet and loveable" as Andre had been taught as boy to believe. While he makes revisions in the way Christ views him, Dubus does not waver in his conviction that God is protecting him, as many of his fictional characters likewise believe. Even those who make no mention of God oftentimes feel as if they are being watched over, not judged, but simply perceived as a parent watches silently, lovingly over a child.

"Running," also from *Broken Vessels,* provides the same sort of reassurance and serves as an allegory for painfully pushing through the difficulties of living, of finding one's center in the most intense and terrifying moments. The essay ends with Dubus's recollection of a father's fear both for himself and for his daughter when the two, out for a hike in the mountains, are caught unaware by a violent thunderstorm. The short, tightly controlled sentences masterfully render the intensity of the scene. When the two catch a ride with a family from Brooklyn who are in peril because of the "terrified" driver's poor skills, the daughter's calm voice works in contrast to their fear. "My father's a good driver," she promises, as he takes over the wheel. Steering steadily, he drives them to safety, an allegory for Christ's love, his vigilance a constant assurance that "Everything will be alright," just as "the father said" (14).

Dubus has been called an existential writer by critics such as Thomas Kennedy, who see at the heart of his work a consistent concern with "an existential Christian vision of a world which human beings must live in, a temporal span which, being alive, they must traverse, and within which they must act. . . . [and] ultimately [are free to] define their own spiritual essence. But always in relation to the new commandment: That we love the human beings with whom we share the world" ("Existential" 91, 101). For Dubus, such labels were laughable: "I never have known what Existentialism meant," he claimed. "Jack [Herlihy, Dubus's personal assistant] told me, 'Here's a definition you can use: 'The existentialist believes that he is doomed to choice.' I said, 'What the hell did people ever think that they were doomed to?'" (Edenfield 144). Kennedy sees that within this ability to choose comes moral responsibility, and equal to that, and equally important to the mind and the work of Andre Dubus, is his awareness of death, that "we are all terminally ill, each breath and step and day one closer to the last," as he writes in "On Charon's Wharf" (*Broken Vessels* 77). This understanding makes each moment a gift, and though he admitted to losing sight of this fact, he credited the sacraments, particularly the sacrament of the Eucharist, for reminding him of the temporal, which in turn made him grateful for each day: "I believe I can approach the altar on any morning of any day which may be the last and receive though that does not, for me, say: There is no death; but does say: In this instant I recognize, with you, that you must die. . . . and it is everything" (78–79). Therefore, he professes, each moment that we live in absolute awareness can become for the participant a sacrament. These moments, these "rituals" shared with others are ultimately what save us from "the lonely price of not living fully in the world" (81). For Dubus, this "living fully in the world" means striving to live peacefully, harmoniously with those we love, knowing that we will fail again and again, yet remain capable always of redemption through everyday acts of affection.

This "living fully" is not easy, as he willingly admitted. In comparing the isolation of housewives to the solitude inherent in his own profession, Dubus commended their bravery in facing the monotony of each day, as he concluded in his essay "Of Robin Hood and Womanhood": "These women, like writers, have no time clocks to punch, no waiting boss. . . . We already are where we have to be, facing ourselves. Both of us, without the prodding of a paycheck or the loss of a job, face only time itself, and our responsibility to use it as best we can" (*Broken Vessels* 54). As with all of Dubus's work, this truth extends beyond his immediate subject as he subtly reminds each of his readers, no matter their gender or profession, of the blessing of each minute we are alive.

He admitted with humor that his early romantic notions regarding women were initially shaped by his boyhood in Louisiana and his love of *Robin Hood,* not the movie version with "Errol Flynn, the Robin Hood who caused too much emotional swirl. . . . [Rather, it was] the book that moved me to the sort of angelic devotion to the female, which is finally a form of exclusion" (57). Fortunately, his experiences as a writer ultimately taught him that not all women need protection like "distant cousins . . . making a fragile visit from the mental institutions where they spend their lives" (56). He self-deprecatingly accounted his chivalric attitude toward his sisters and their friends, who could not help but be amused by his acts of deference. In time, however, he learned and relearned "to erase the old boundaries, to see women as they are and I suppose always were: creatures like me, who live in the same world I live in" (58).

This kind of awareness made Dubus grateful for the simple act of taking a breath, as he explained in the essay "Breathing," of being "absolutely in the present" by focusing "only on breathing" (156). While this lesson came fully to the writer on his hospital bed at Massachusetts General as nurses and doctors worked to stop a hemorrhage in his left leg, many of his fictional characters had gotten there before him as, aware of their every movement, they take stock of their every blessing. This awareness, of being fully in the moment, is ultimately grace, as he explains in the essay titled "Grace" in *Meditations from a Moveable Chair* and again in "Sacraments": "I am receiving sacraments with each breath, as I did while I slept; with each movement of my body" (87). Again, in "Bodily Mysteries" Dubus found relief from despair, relief from the "isolation only the human soul has to endure," as he wrote in "Sacraments." This isolation was caused, he suspected, by forgetting that "we are always receiving sacraments" (87). Such loneliness could be alleviated for Dubus and for others in his fictional world who remember that we are "one with all people in pain and joy and passion, one with the physical universe, with Christ, with the timeless dimension of the spirit, which has no past or future, but only now; one with God. Me: flawed and foolish me" ("Bodily Mysteries" 101–2). For Dubus, redemption came in the awareness of each moment and in personal responsibility to others, in spite of how often one might fail. Nevertheless, these blessings come to us in spite of our distractedness, he explained in the essay "Communion," dedicated to his grandson Austin Dubus and collected in *Meditations from a Moveable Chair.* We receive "with wandering minds, and distracted flesh, in the same way that we receive the sun and sky, the moon and earth, and breathing" (159). The characters in Dubus's fiction who feel the most peace find it through this absolute awareness of the earth and of another, knowing that the beloved is temporal and therefore all the more precious.

That life is fleeting, each second a gift, was made manifest in Dubus's life on the night of July 23, 1986, a horrifying near-death, but life-affirming experience for the writer, recounted in detail by many interviewers but never so well as by the author himself, as he did in the essay "Lights of the Long Night." Without blame or pity, Dubus concluded, "I am forever a cripple, but I am alive, and I am a father and a husband, and in 1987 I am sitting in the sunlight of June and writing this" (*Broken Vessels* 131). "Carrying," from *Meditations from a Moveable Chair,* extends this celebration of familial love. The essay tells of an afternoon in June when his family came together to celebrate with his daughter Cadence, who was turning ten. The immediacy of his joy is enhanced by his use of the present tense. When the party moves off the deck and onto the grass, his son and namesake, Andre III, offers to carry his father down the stairs, where he can join the family on the lawn, where he has not ventured for six years. The moment is fraught with Dubus's admitted fear "of falling, of being paralyzed. And being carried frightens me in ways I cannot name; perhaps the absolute surrender to another human being dramatizes for me the dangers I can no longer ward off or evade." Dubus's characters confront many such moments, of choosing to surrender with the faith that those they love will not "drop" them. "I say yes" (113), and his oldest son "encircles" his father, takes him safely to earth and turns his chair "to face the sun" (114). Dubus takes in the day, the "shadows that darken the wetlands across the road," the sun "behind the trees, the sky at their crowns rose and orange" (114–15). Time is passing, the day is moving on, but he is in the moment, sustained by his family and their abiding love.

Despair would return, as he explained in the collection's title and final essay. Yet he learned to live again, damaged, broken, never the same "vessel," but a new one, transformed by pain and reconstructed by the many acts of kindness shown to him by friends and family, who tended his every need with love. In "a time of spiritual pain," he wrote in "A Hemingway Story," he dreamt of the writer whom he "thought very often of . . . and how much physical pain he had suffered, and how well he had written about it" (54). In the dream, Hemingway comes to him, walking across the lawn and into his kitchen through the screen door: "He wore his fishing cap with a long visor. He walked straight to me and said: 'Let's go fishing' . . . [The next evening] sitting in my chair in the quiet night, I believed that Hemingway had come to me while I was suffering and had taken me away from it, out to sea, where we could fish" (54–55). Many such comforting acts are recounted in "Broken Vessels," an essay of such length that it is given its own section in the collection, a revealing point. While long, the piece never drags, never dips into unwarranted sentiments, just as his stories never do. In fact, the essay ends allegorically, as his fiction often does, leaving the reader with a clearer understanding of what it means to be alive and happy in the moments we are given. In July 1988 his daughter Cadence, just six years old, has been practicing with her father's chair, moving through the house as her father did, maneuvering with difficulty up and down the ramps: "*Now I know what it's like to be you,*" she told her father (194). She inherited his gift for empathy, the need to see the world from another's perspective, to live life with his or her limitations, hard as it may be.

This is the true brilliance of the work of Andre Dubus, his ability to provide with dignity and without judgment the myriad points of view of limited, flawed human beings struggling both tragically and heroically to navigate their complicated worlds, worlds very much like his own: a "landscape made up of obstacles and traps," as Wolff noted (*Broken Vessels* xvii). The essays make the fiction more personal, the voice more immediate, though the themes remain the same, the experience just as sweet.

NOTES

Chapter 1: Understanding Andre Dubus

1. Dubus would remain loyal to his connections at Godine until 1996, when he was forced by monetary concerns to switch to Alfred A. Knopf of New York, which published his last collection of short stories, *Dancing After Hours* (1996), as well as his second collection of essays, *Meditations from a Moveable Chair* (1998).

2. As Dubus admitted to Edenfield, "I have some autobiographical stories about my boyhood. . . . When I wrote the stories about a boy named Clement, I used actual events." However, the stories are "my adult memory of my childhood perceptions of someone I've never really known" (145).

Chapter 2: Boyhood and Military Life

1. Dubus would confess to Kay Bonetti that his insecurity over his own small boyhood frame made him self-conscious and insecure: "I was little, and I wasn't a good athlete. And in the fifties that meant you don't get a girl. . . . It's my image of myself" (Edenfield 57).

2. Patrick Samway gives a fair account of Richie's mother, Joan, who, on the one hand is grateful for her past and for her children at the same time that she opts "not to resume a life where risks are undertaken for the sake of potential growth" ("Dubus's *Voices*" 80–81). To avoid the possibilities of sin, Richie is close to becoming sealed off like his mother. Melissa is in fact Richie's salvation, his way into the world.

3. The responsibilities of fatherhood sometimes lead his protagonists to commit crimes that only few regret. Matt Fowler from "Killings" knows that he has committed a murder that will divide him from his former self just as it will create a wall between himself and his wife, though he will never admit it to anyone. Vocalizing his regret will only make Ruth's suffering worse.

4. Dubus was frank about a military wife's obligation to her husband's profession, telling Bonetti, "it's 'we' in the military; it is 'we.' [My wife] was in the Marine Corps, too" (Edenfield 57).

Chapter 3: Women and Domestic Space

1. Dubus admitted that Juanita "is going to commit suicide. That's her isolation. She says that she feels like she's sneaking into a movie. . . . that's why I call that 'Waiting,' because she's going to do it. I mean, you know, she went out in the goddamn Pacific at night" (Edenfield 171).

2. Junkins convincingly argues that the opening paragraph of "Cat in the Rain" "functions as a cryptic description (archetypes of war monuments, artists, tourists, sea,

doorways, empty square, etc.) and as a foreshadowing of the explicit statement of the woman trapped in a kind of spiritual and perhaps physical neglect" (19).

3. Dubus was asked by many interviewers about the various allusions in "Miranda over the Valley." While he was always forthcoming in his responses, he was also suspicious of teachers who "get a little weird with that stuff" (Edenfield 147).

BIBLIOGRAPHY

Books by Andre Dubus

COLLECTIONS OF SHORT FICTION

Adultery and Other Choices. Boston: David R. Godine, 1977. Contents: "An Afternoon with the Old Man," "Contrition," "The Bully," "Graduation," "The Fat Girl," "Cadence," "Corporal of Artillery," "The Shooting," "Andromache," "Adultery."

Dancing After Hours. New York: Alfred A. Knopf, 1996. Contents: "The Intruder," "A Love Song," "Falling in Love," "Blessings," "Sunday Morning," "All the Time in the World," "Woman on a Plane," "The Colonel's Wife," "The Lover," "The Last Moon," "The Timing of Sin," "At Night," "Out of the Snow," "Dancing After Hours."

Finding a Girl in America: A Novella and Ten Short Stories. Boston: David R. Godine, 1980. Contents: "Killings," "The Dark Men," "His Lover," "Townies," "The Misogamist," "At St. Croix," 'The Pitcher," "Waiting," "Delivering," "The Winter Father," "Finding a Girl in America."

In the Bedroom. New York: Vintage Contemporaries, 2002. Contents: "Killings," "The Winter Father," "Rose," "The Fat Girl," "Delivering," "A Father's Story," "All the Time in the World."

The Last Worthless Evening: Four Novellas and Two Stories. Boston: David R. Godine, 1986. Contents: "Deaths at Sea," "After the Game," "Dressed Like Summer Leaves," "Land Where My Fathers Died," "Molly," "Rose."

Separate Flights: A Novella and Seven Short Stories. Boston: David R. Godine, 1975. Contents: "We Don't live Here Anymore," "Over the Hill," "The Doctor," "In My Life," "If They Knew Yvonne," "Going Under," "Miranda over the Valley," "Separate Flights."

The Times Are Never So Bad: A Novella and Eight Short Stories. Boston: David R. Godine, 1983. Contents: "The Pretty Girl," "Bless Me, Father," "Goodbye," "Leslie in California," "The New Boy," "The Captain," "Sorrowful Mysteries," "Anna," "A Father's Story."

We Don't Live Here Anymore: The Novellas of Andre Dubus. New York: Crown Publishers, 1984. Contents: "The Pretty Girl," "We Don't Live Here Anymore," "Adultery," "Finding a Girl in America."

NOVELLA

Land Where My Fathers Died. Winston-Salem, N.C.: Palaemon Press, 1985. Limited edition.

NOVELS

The Lieutenant. New York: Dial Press, 1967.
Voices from the Moon. Boston: David R. Godine, 1984.

COLLECTIONS OF ESSAYS

Broken Vessels. Boston: David R. Godine, 1991. Contents: "Out Like a Lamb," "Running," "Under the Lights," "The End of a Season," "Railroad Sketches," "Of Robin Hood and Womanhood," "The Judge and Other Snakes," "On Charon's Wharf," "After Twenty Years," "Into the Silence," "A Salute to Mr. Yates," "Selling Stories," "Marketing," "Two Ghosts," "Intensive Care," "Lights of the Long Night," "Sketches at Home," "A Woman in April," "Bastille Day," "Husbands," "Breathing," "Broken Vessels."

Meditations from a Moveable Chair. New York: Alfred A. Knopf, 1998. Contents: "About Kathryn," "Legs," "Letter to a Writer's Workshop," "Digging," Imperiled Men," "A Hemingway Story," "Grace," "Mailer at the Algonquin," "Brothers," "Good-bye to Richard Yates," "Sacraments," "Bodily Mysteries," "A Country Road Song," "Carrying," "Girls," "Liv Ullmann in Spring," "Love in the Morning," "Song of Pity," "Communion," "First Books," "Letter to Amtrak," "Autumn Legs," "Giving up the Gun," "Messages," "Witness."

EDITED VOLUME

Into the Silence: American Stories. Cambridge, Mass.: Green Street Press, 1988.

SHORT FICTION (UNCOLLECTED)

"The Blackberry Patch." In *Southern Writing in the Sixties: Fiction.* Edited by John William Corrington and Miller Williams. Baton Rouge: Louisiana State University Press, 1966. 108–15. Reprinted in *Stories of the Modern South.* Edited by Benjamin Forkner and Patrick Samway, S.J. New York: Bantam, 1978. 78–83.

"Love Is the Sky." *Midwestern University Quarterly* 2.2 (1966): 18–32.

"Madeline Sheppard." *Midwestern University Quarterly* 2.4 (1967): 1–12.

"Riding North." *Oxford Magazine* 12 (Spring/Summer 1998): 92–120.

"Sisters." *Book,* May–June 1999: 53–60.

Secondary Sources

Anderson, Donald, ed. *Andre Dubus: Tributes.* New Orleans: Xavier Review Press, 2001.

"Andre Dubus: Storytelling, Part of His Art." *Dialogue,* October 14, 1985: 3.

Baker, James N. Review of *Adultery and Other Choices. Newsweek,* December 5, 1977: 100.

Benzel, Kathryn Nowicki. "Sexual Difference as Narrative Technique: Cross-Dressing, Redressing, and Undressing Female Protagonists." *Dissertation Abstracts International* 49.1 (1988): 88A.

Bodwell, Joshua. "The Art of Reading Andre Dubus: We Don't Have to Live Great Lives." *Poets and Writers* 36.4 (2008): 21–25.

Brennan, Matthew C. "The 'Flow' of the Game: Andre Dubus' 'The Pitcher.'" *Nine: A Journal of Baseball History and Social Policy Perspectives* 8.2 (2000): 114–22.

Breslin, John B. "Andre Dubus, R.I.P." *Commonweal* 126.8 (1999): 10.

———. "Playing out the Patterns of Sin and Grace: The Catholic Imagination of Andre Dubus." *Commonweal* 115 (1988): 652–56.

Brown, Suzanne Hunter. "Andre Dubus (1936–1999)." *Columbia Companion to the Twentieth-Century American Short Story* (2000): 226–34.

Broyard, Anatole. Review of *Adultery and Other Choices. New York Times Book Review,* November 20, 1977: 14.

Busch, Frederick. "Andre Dubus 1936–1999." In *Published and Perished: Memoria, Eulogies, and Remembrances of American Writers.* Edited by Steven Gilbar and Dean Stewart. Boston: Godine, 2002. 200–202.

Cassidy, Thomas, and Charles E. May. "Andre Dubus." *Critical Survey of Short Fiction.* 2nd ed. New York: Salem Press, 2001,1–4.

Cocchiarale, Michael. "The Complicated Catholicism of Andre Dubus." In *Songs of the New South: Writing Contemporary Louisiana.* Edited by Suzanne Disherron Green and Lisa Abbey. Westport, Conn.: Greenwood, 2001. 107–14.

Cohen, Michael. "Agonists of the Contemporary Memoir." *Missouri Review* 31.2 (2008): 174–87.

Contino, Paul J. "Andre Dubus's Eucharistic Imagination." *Religion and the Arts* 6.1–2 (2002): 52–72.

Cox, Shelly. Review of *The Times Are Never So Bad. Library Journal* 108 (July 1983): 1380.

Cryer, Dan. "Andre Dubus: Ironic Stories on Timeless Themes." *Newsday,* November 30, 1986: 20.

Devlin, James E. "Andre Dubus." *American Short-Story Writers since World War II.* Detroit: Thomson Gale, 1993. 142–49.

Doherty, Paul. "'Heroism' and 'Ordinary Life' in the Stories of Andre Dubus." *Religion and the Arts* 6.1–2 (2002): 149–62.

Doyle, Brian. "A Graceful Man: Andre Dubus, 1936–1999." *U.S. Catholic* 64.11 (1999): 36–37.

Dubus, Kathryn, and Vaughan B. Simpson. Personal interview by author. October 16, 2013.

Edenfield, Olivia Carr, ed. *Conversations with Andre Dubus.* Jackson: University Press of Mississippi, 2013.

Ermelino, Louisa. "My Dinner with Andre." *Publishers Weekly* 255.17 (2008): 106.

Escuret, Annie. "Une nouvelle d'Andre Dubus: 'The Doctor' ou le pont, le flot et l'enfant." *Delta* 24 (February 1987): 109–26.

Feeney, Joseph J. "Poised for Fame: Andre Dubus at Fifty." *America,* November 15, 1986: 296–99.

Ferriss, Lucy. "'Never Truly Members.'" In *Southern Writers at Century's End.* Edited by Jeffrey J. Folks and James A. Perkins. Lexington: University Press of Kentucky, 1997. 226–37.

Flamm, Matthew, "Talking with Andre Dubus." *Newsday,* April 14, 1996: C31+.

Forbes, Cheryl. "Writing the Body: An Experiment in Material Rhetoric." *Rhetoric Review* 19.1–2 (2000): 60–72.

Fryer, Judith. *Felicitous Space: The Imaginative Structures of Edith Wharton and Willa Cather.* Chapel Hill: University of North Carolina Press, 1986.

Gaudet, Marcia. "Catholic Palimpsest: The Louisiana Stories of Andre Dubus." *Xavier Review* 23.1 (2003): 44–57.

Gies, Judith. "Little Voices." *Village Voice,* November 26–December 2, 1980: 42.

Gilbert, Harriett. "States of Desire." *New Statesman* 108.2799 (November 9, 1984): 32.

Gleason, Edward, ed. *Andre Dubus/Andre Dubus III*. Special issue of *Xavier Review* 30.2 (2010): 1–165.

———. "Horses Running Back into the Fire and Other Self-Immolations in 'A Father's Story.'" *Religion and the Arts* 6.1–2 (2002): 175–86.

Godine, David R. Personal interview by author. April 7, 2015.

Goldsmith, Jeff. "*We Don't Live Here Anymore*." *Creative Screenwriting* 11.4 (2005): 34–35.

Gornick, Vivian. "Tenderhearted Men: Lonesome, Sad and Blue." *New York Times Book Review,* September 16, 1990: 1, 32–36.

Gray, Paul. "Loners and Losers." Review of *The Last Worthless Evening. Time,* November 10, 1986: 59.

———. Review of *The Times Are Never So Bad, Time,* August 15, 1983: 61.

Gresham, Ross, ed. *Leap of the Heart: Andre Dubus Talking.* Xavier Review Press, 2003.

Grubgeld, Elizabeth. "Body, Privacy, and Community: Reading Disability in the Late Fiction of Andre Dubus." *Religion and the Arts* 39.2 (2007): 33–53.

———. "A Dangerous Harbor: Andre Dubus, Walker Percy, and Marriage." *Xavier Review* 30.2 (2010): 58–73.

———. "Living on the Invisible Palm of God: Andre Dubus and the Ethics of Forceful Resistance." *Religion and the Arts* 6.1–2 (2002): 19–35.

Hammond, David M. "Identity, Community and Choice in Andre Dubus's 'Miranda Over the Valley.'" *Religion and the Arts* 6.1–2 (2002): 163–74.

Hanley, Brian. "Andre Dubus: A Survey of Research and Criticism." *Resources for American Literary Study* 28 (2003): 1–16.

Harris, Michael. "Love's Limitations." *Washington Post Book World,* July 20, 1975: 3.

Hubert, Thomas. "The Louisiana Connection in the Fiction of Andre Dubus." *McNeese Review* 26 (1979–80): 74–81.

Ivanov, Andrea. "Doing Penance in the Old West: 'Sisters' as Andre Dubus's Final Word on Suffering Rape." *Renascence* 60.3 (2008): 251–69.

Junkins, Donald. "Hemingway's Contribution to American Poetry" *Hemingway Review* 4.2 (1985): 18–23.

Kelly, Lionel. "American Fat: Obesity and the Short Story." *Yearbook of English Studies* 31 (2001): 218–29.

Kennedy, Thomas E. *Andre Dubus: A Study of the Short Fiction*. Boston: Twayne, 1988.

———. "The Existential Christian Vision in the Fiction of Andre Dubus." *Delta* 24 (February 1987): 91–102.

———. "A Fiction of People and Events." *Sewanee Review* 95.2 (Spring 1987): xxxix–xli.

———. "The First and Last Stories of Andre Dubus." *Gettysburg Review* 14.2 (2001): 229–36.

———. "The Progress from Hunger to Love: Three Novellas by Andre Dubus." *Hollins Critic* 24 (February 1987): 1–9.

———. "Sweet Fire: Memories of Andre Dubus." *Agni* 50 (1999): 179–88.

Krieger, Elliot. "Andre Dubus Suffered for His Commitment." *Providence Sunday Journal,* December 21, 1986: I-7.

Lacy, Robert. "The House on Brown Street." *Sewanee Review* 112.4 (2004): 583–91.

———. "Richard Yates in Iowa." *Sewanee Review* 118.3 (2010): 422–28.

Lesser, Ellen. "Going the Distance." *Village Voice,* January 20, 1987: 50, 52.

Levine, Judith. Review of *The Times Are Never So Bad. Village Voice Literary Supplement,* February 23, 1984: 3–4.

Lewis, Robert P. "'No More Male and Female': Bodiliness and Eucharist in Andre Dubus's Stories." *Religion and the Arts* 6.1–2 (2002): 36–51.

———. "Anamnesis: Andre Dubus's Catholic Imagination." *Religion and the Arts* 4.2 (2000): 247–59.

Lyons, Bonnie, and Bill Oliver. "Passion Is Better." In *Passion and Craft: Conversations with Notable Writers.* Urbana: University of Illinois Press, 1998. 145–58.

Lyons, Gene. "Eavesdropping on the Quotidian." Review of *Separate Flights. Nation,* February 26, 1977: 248–50.

———. Review of *The Times Are Never So Bad. Newsweek,* July 18, 1983: 70.

Masinton, Charles G. "Stories Celebrate Strengths of Ordinary People." *Kansas City Star,* March 22, 1987.

Massey, Doreen. *Space, Place, and Gender.* Minneapolis: University of Minnesota Press, 1994.

Max, Daniel. "Dubus an Unknown Master." *Chicago Tribune,* January 22, 1987: D-3.

McFarlane, Brian. "Shooting Minds." *Meanjin* 64.3 (2005): 216–22.

Mergendahl, Peter. Review of *The Last Worthless Evening. Rocky Mountain News Sunday Magazine,* 31.

Milton, Edith. Review of *Adultery and Other Choices. New Republic,* February 4, 1978: 33–35.

Miner, Madonne. "'Jumping from One Heart to Another': How Andre Dubus Writes about Women." *Critique: Studies in Contemporary Fiction* 39.1 (1997): 18–31.

———. "'Making up the Stories as We Go Along': Men, Women, and Narratives of Disability." In *The Body and Physical Difference: Discourses of Disability.* Edited by David T. Mitchell and Sharon L. Snyder. Ann Arbor: University of Michigan Press, 1997. 283–95.

———. "'The Seirênês Will Sing His Mind Away': Andre Dubus's 'The Curse.'" *Studies in Short Fiction* 31.3 (1994): 397–406.

———. "What Cannot Be Told: Gender and the Limits of Storytelling in Andre Dubus's 'Graduation.'" *Critique: Studies in Contemporary Fiction* 44.3 (2003): 227–35.

Moynahan, Julian. "Hard Lives." Review of *Finding a Girl in America. New York Times Book Review,* June 22, 1980: 12.

Oates, Joyce Carol, "People to Whom Things Happen." Review of *The Times Are Never So Bad. New York Times Book Review,* June 26, 1983: 12, 18.

———. Review of *Separate Flights. Ontario Review,* Fall–Winter 1976–77: 105–6.

O'Donnell, Brennan. "'Mysteries of Love and Mortality' in Andre Dubus's 'Adultery' and 'On Charon's Wharf.'" *Religion and the Arts* 6.1–2 (2002): 113–29.

O'Donnell, Brennan, Paul J. Contino, and Jane Kelley Rodeheffer, eds. *The Work of Andre Dubus.* Special issue of *Religion and the Arts* 6.1–2 (2002): 1–230.

Olson, Clarence. "Life's Litany of Flaws." *St. Louis Post Dispatch,* December 14, 1986: 5-J.

Osteen, Mark. "Ritual and Reenactment in Andre Dubus's Short Fiction." *Religion and the Arts* 6.1-2 (2002): 73-89.

Peck, Elizabeth G. "More Than Ideal: Size and Weight Obsession in Literary Works by Marge Piercy, Margaret Atwood, and Andre Dubus." *Platte Valley Review* 18.1 (1990): 69–75.

Penner, Jonathan. "The Making of a Storyteller." *Washington Post Book World,* December 18, 1977: E7.

Posesorski, Sherie. "Exploring Places in the Heart." *Boston Herald,* November 23, 1986: 57–58.

Raynor, Janice. Review of *The Last Worthless Evening. Worcester Sunday Telegraph,* January 18, 1987: 12D.

Review of *Finding a Girl in America. Choice* 18 (December 1980): 526.

Robison, James C. "1969–1980: Experiment and Tradition." In *The American Short Story 1945–1980: A Critical History.* Edited by Gordon Weaver. Boston: Twayne, 1983. 102.

Rosser, Phyllis. "There's No Place Like Home." In *New Feminist Criticism: Art, Identity, Action.* Edited by Joanna Fruch, Cassandra L. Langer, and Arlene Raven. New York: IconEditions, 1994. 60–79.

Rowe, Anne E. "Andre Dubus (1936–)." *Contemporary Fiction Writers of the South: A Bio-Bibliographical Sourcebook.* Westport, Conn.: Greenwood, 1993. 101–11.

Samway, Patrick J. "Dubus's *Voices from the Moon:* More Mystery and Manners." *Delta* 24 (February 1987): 78–90.

———. "Pilgrims and Prophets: The Figure of the Priest in the Fiction of Andre Dubus and Walker Percy." *Image: A Journal of the Arts and Religion* 24 (1999): 93–104.

Samway, Patrick, Gordon O. Taylor, and Monroe Engel. "Religion and Writing." *Wilson Quarterly* 19.3 (1995): 158–59.

Shands, Kerstin W. *Embracing Space: Spatial Metaphors in Feminist Discourse.* Westport, Conn.: Greenwood, 1999.

———. "I Can See Them There, at Fenway Park—Andre Dubus and His Good Friend God . . ."

Religion and the Arts 6.1–2 (2002): 5–18.

Shreve, Anita. "The American Short Story: An Untold Tale." *New York Times,* November 30, 1980: sec. 6, 136.

Sigal, Clancy. "A Hero in the Worst of Us." Review of *The Last Worthless Evening. New York Times Book Review,* December 21, 1986: 12.

Soete, Mary. Review of *Adultery and Other Choices. Library Journal,* January 15, 1978: 191.

———. Review of *Finding a Girl in America. Library Journal,* June 15, 1980: 1408.

Stonehill, Brian. "Memory, the Lens to Look at Life." Review of *The Times Are Never So Bad. Los Angeles Times Book Review.* August 14, 1983: 5.

Sullivan, Jack. Review of *Adultery and Other Choices. Saturday Review,* January 21, 1978: 50.

———. "The Way We Live Now: The Fiction of Andre Dubus." *Washington Post Book World,* January 11, 1987: 7.

Sullivan, Walter J. Review of *Separate Flights. Sewanee Review* (Summer 1975): 544–46.

Swanson, William. "Everyday Survivors." *Ambassador* (TWA magazine), October 1985: 90, 92–94, 98.

Taliaferro, Frances. Review of *Adultery and Other Choices. Harper's,* January 1978: 87.

Taylor, Robert. Review of *The Last Worthless Evening. Boston Globe,* November 19, 1986: 75.

Updike, John. "Ungreat Lives." Review of *Voices from the Moon. New Yorker,* February 4, 1985: 94–101.

Vauthier, S. "Au-dela du réalisme: 'Sorrowful Mysteries.'" *Delta* 24 (February 1987): 127–50.

Wendorf, Thomas A. "Erotic and Divine Love: Implications of the Incarnation in Dubus's 'If They Knew Yvonne,' *Voices from the Moon*, and 'Adultery.'" *Religion and the Arts* 6.1–2 (2002): 131–48.

Whittaker, S. "Andre Dubus's' 'His Lover' and the Classical Temper." *Delta* 24 (February 1987): 103–8.

Wickenden, Dorothy. Review of *Finding a Girl in America. New Republic,* August 23, 1980: 37.

Yarbrough, Steve. "Andre Dubus: From Detached Incident to Compressed Novel." *Critique: Studies in Contemporary Fiction* 28.1 (1986): 19–27.

Zeidner, Lisa. "Surviving Life." Review of *Voices from the Moon. New York Times Book Review,* November 18, 1984: 26.

INDEX